CCCC Studies in Writing & Rhetoric

# EVERYDAY GENRES

# EVERYDAY GENRES
## WRITING ASSIGNMENTS ACROSS THE DISCIPLINES

Mary Soliday

Southern Illinois University Press
*Carbondale and Edwardsville*

14  13  12  11    4  3  2  1

Publication partially funded by a subvention grant
from the Conference on College Composition and
Communication of the National Council of Teachers
of English.

Library of Congress Cataloging-in-Publication Data
  Soliday, Mary.
  Everyday genres : writing assignments across the dis-
ciplines / Mary Soliday.
      p. cm.—(CCCC studies in writing & rhetoric)
  Includes bibliographical references and index.
  ISBN-13: 978-0-8093-3019-5 (pbk. : alk. paper)
  ISBN-10: 0-8093-3019-9 (pbk. : alk. paper)
  ISBN-13: 978-0-8093-8618-5 (ebook)
  ISBN-10: 0-8093-8618-6 (ebook)
  1. English language—Rhetoric—Study and teaching.
  2. Interdisciplinary approach in education. 3. Language
  arts—Correlation with content subjects. I. Title.
  PE1404.S636 2010
  808'.0420711—dc22            2010020242

*To L. F. Hanley*

# CONTENTS

## PREFACE

*EVERYDAY GENRES* EXPLORES THE WRITING ASSIGNMENTS we encounter in university writing across the curriculum (WAC) programs. In recent years, theorists have argued that genres aren't the sum of their individual conventions as much as they perform typical social actions for readers. Theorists assert also that writers acquire genres in the specific situations of their use. Drawing on apprenticeship models of learning, the theory insists on the socializing power of written genres to hold groups together. In their studies of local situations, scholars document how experts acquire written forms in a dense social context of talking, thinking, reading, and writing. If the goal is to help students to acquire written forms, then it follows that teachers need to build effective social contexts through which a novice writer becomes familiar with the typical motives that create the conventions usually associated with genres.

Genre study also leads composition studies—and WAC—to consider largely unresolved theoretical and institutional questions about the nature of a rhetorical situation, writing ability, and rhetorical expertise. Although students may earn good grades in freshman composition, professors in other disciplines say that in their classes, these same students can't seem to write; these teachers are questioning whether writing can be taught separately from its specific situation. Or when composition scholars wonder whether their models of composing are appropriate for other disciplines, they are asking whether expertise can be shared across situations. In both cases, teachers query to what extent writing is a general, as opposed to a purely situational, ability.

The current book explores these global questions by examining situations from a WAC program I coordinated for seven years at the City College of New York (CCNY). In the program I describe, doctoral students, called writing fellows, were paired with faculty who worked with these fellows so they could improve their teaching in general-education courses, major courses, and some graduate courses. From the outset, I assumed the fellows and I could share our expertise with faculty, but I also learned those of us in WAC needed to have familiarity with the rhetorical situation: the professor's motives for making assignments and some knowledge of a field's content and language. Based on our experiences in WAC, I conclude we can give students better access to specialized genres if we give them access to the social situations of use from which genres draw their power and meaning.

The book's introduction and first chapter provide the theoretical and institutional context for the particular studies of assigned genres offered in the second two chapters. I overview genre theory in the introduction, referring to the apprenticeship model of learning much theory draws from. Chapter 1, "Sharing Genre Expertise," describes how the City University of New York (CUNY) writing-fellows program was established and then developed at CCNY, one of seventeen colleges in the municipal system that was mandated to develop a WAC program. Chapter 2, "Stance in Genre," considers a major problem students identify in university writing: how to develop an appropriate stance to talk about evidence to expert readers. Chapter 3, "Content in Genre," examines the related challenge of how novice writers find information and then shape their content into evidence for expert readers. Briefly in the conclusion, I complicate apprenticeship models of learning that exclude reflective thinking about rhetorical purpose and conventional forms.

Like many scholars who came to composition studies with literary backgrounds, my understanding of how to gain permission from students to cite their words, spoken or written, has evolved along with the field's. I used an in-house form to document students' permission until the spring of 2002, when I was first introduced to the campus Institutional Review Board (IRB) and protocols for conducting human-subjects research. Accordingly, the material I cite in this book reflects this evolution. The teacher research the fellows conducted before the fall of 2002 was not approved by the IRB, though students gave fellows their permission to cite their words. Most students in selected classes gave permission to use their written work for outside readers to evaluate, but we never interviewed representative numbers of students in any class. In most cases, students received stipends to participate in interviews, as did the outside readers, who scored essays in a study of a music class, and teaching assistants interviewed in a study of a psychology class. I've given pseudonyms to all students to protect their confidentiality. Over the course of three separate reviews, the IRB did not require me to obtain consent from faculty or fellows, although by 2006, when I finished my studies, they had phased in such a requirement. In the absence of an IRB protocol, I've referred to the fellows and to the faculty by pseudonyms.

Institutional voices are central to this book because it is by listening to teaching assistants, doctoral candidates, professors, and undergraduates that I understand why WAC programs are so vital to sustain in higher education today. I recall one undergraduate who asserted, in an interview, that she had to learn to write all over again for every situation she encountered in college because professors' motives and preferences ("what they want") always change. To a certain extent, this is true, and her insight, widely shared by students in other institutions, illuminates the close relationship between writing and situation that genre study addresses. At the same time, I suggest that general principles of rhetoric probably do transfer across situations, but the only way students can grasp the transfer is if their professors share some common approaches to the teaching of writing. WAC directors often tell faculty that the responsibility for teaching writing rests with them, but perhaps it's more proper to say, finally, that it rests with our institutions.

## ACKNOWLEDGMENTS

WAC PROGRAMS ALWAYS INVOLVE a large cast of characters too numerous to name, but I need to try. Over many years, Dean Paul Sherwin, Ellen Smiley, Dean Judith Summerfield, and Josh Wilner have, in their administrative roles, supported my efforts to build writing programs. The Eisner Research Foundation at City College awarded me a release from teaching in fall 2007. Across five boroughs, City University of New York colleagues made me a better WAC scholar: Marian Arkin, Michael Cripps, Hugh English, Peter Gray, Linda Hirsch, Nancy Lester, Mark McBeth, Linda Stanley, and, especially, Kate Garretson. I worked with a stellar group of talented writing fellows, among them Eliza Darling, Elsa Davidson, Alina Gharabegian, Erin Henriksen, Brenda Henry-Offor, Russell Hogg, Young-Mi Lim, Tim McCormack, Kathleen Nolan, Rachel Nuger, Binh Pok, Camille Tipton, and Rob Wallace; a special shout-out to Debbie Wolf. Professors like Bill Behnken, Deborah Coates, Ed Keller, Dan Lemons, Elizabeth Starcevik, Diana Wall, Gay Wilgus, and many others made me believe that teachers in the disciplines teach writing as well as English professors do. Reviewers Beverly Moss and Carol Rutz and, especially, Joe Harris read this manuscript more than once with critical care and genuine concern. Larry Hanley continues to advance all my knowledge. Finally, the City College of New York was a truly amazing place to work because of the faculty's dedication, made obvious in this book, to a richly diverse group of students who, over seventeen years, taught me more than they will ever know.

EVERYDAY GENRES

# Introduction

EVERYDAY GENRES CONCERNS WRITING ASSIGNMENTS professors give
their students on a daily basis. Every day in the university, teachers
ask students to write dissertations and research papers, critical essays
and lab reports. The quality of these genres may determine grades
and institutional credentials and entry to or exit from a variety of
programs. Professors use them to assess the writer's intellectual grasp
of material, and, through written genres, some students experience
the most direct contact with university experts they will enjoy. In
this book, I assume these everyday school forms are (or could be)
no less a situated writing practice than professional or workplace
genres, because their acquisition has important consequences for
generations of writers.

The scientific article professors write and sometimes assign to
their students provides an example of a consequential rhetorical
form with a long and complex cultural history. Ordinary genres
like the article and its humble cousin the lab report play powerful
roles in sustaining our disciplines because, Mikhail Bakhtin argued
decades ago, their typical words carry with them significant ethi-
cal and social values and ways of being in the world. More recent
studies of how genres originate, such as Michael McKeon's important study of the early-modern English novel, show they evolve and
endure because they fulfill the cultural needs Bakhtin describes.
Charles Bazerman documents how, also during this early-modern
period, the scientific article evolved to express and shape the new
social structures of the scientific enterprise (*Shaping*). The scientific
article students read and sometimes write has long served and still
does serve broad ideological, social, and epistemological purposes
for readers in academic culture.

If asked, most teachers and students would probably say everyday genres are the sum of their specific textual conventions. In my

experience, teachers tend to think an essay is, above all, marked by coherence: the main point given up front; smooth transitional sentences between paragraphs. Students I've known use the word *flow* to describe this salient convention of the college-essay genre. But though we do recognize a genre through its conventions, a genre does not achieve power and durability exclusively through an inventory of its textual features. For years now, theorists have told us that genres exceed their conventions because, as I argue in this book, they perform meaningful social actions for readers. In the university, the workplace, or anywhere writing occurs, genres shape how writers typically speak about something in response to a recurring situation. Genre shapes how writers talk *about* something to someone *for some reason*.

In her landmark essay, "Genre as Social Action," Carolyn Miller points out that if genre represents action, "it must involve situation and motive, because human action, whether symbolic or otherwise, is interpretable only against a context of situation and through the attributing of motives" (152). Through genre, "a rhetorical practice," readers and writers (or speakers and listeners) respond to repeated situations in typical ways (155). However, though we use genre to respond to recurrent situations, it is not the form itself that is conventionalized as much as the "social purpose" it responds to and helps to realize (162; see also Miller, "Rhetorical Community"). Everyday school genres do important educational and cultural work because they embody and help to sustain the basic functioning of social groups (Bawarshi; Berkenkotter and Huckin; Bhatia; Christie and Martin; Cope and Kalantzis; Freedman and Medway, *Genre and the New Rhetoric*; Miller, "Rhetorical Community"; Paltridge). Therefore, genre study brings to WAC an important insistence on the socializing power of everyday assignments. Amy Devitt puts the case especially well: "Genres function for people in their interactions with one another in groups and through social structures; they are social actions" (34).

Genre is a *social practice* through which writers interact with readers. As a social practice, genre links the expectations of individual readers and writers to those of larger social groups. By expectations, I mean a group's typical words (or, in Bakhtin's terms, social languages) and their typical perceptions, beliefs, values, and core concepts. To master a genre, a novice has to interact with readers in some way, gaining a sense of how these expectations shape the situation and of how readers attribute motives to written forms. Therefore, writers in university situations must learn what constitutes a typical, as opposed to an imitative, expression. Typicality has not been a popular subject for writing teachers because it smacks of formalism and, perhaps, threatens our deeply held disciplinary sense that each text is original or belongs to the writer. But, genre asks us to consider how a reader's expectations constrain the rhetorical situation and powerfully shape any writing task. This book focuses on two areas of typicality involving stance and content. In the first area, I examine how writers present their material or what stance they take on it. In the second, I focus on what counts as evidence for readers, and on what writers do with their content for readers. To say it another way, I focus on how writers appropriately present something that counts as evidence for their readers.

The following chapters examine the genres teachers assigned in the WAC program at the City College of New York (CCNY), a senior college in the City University of New York (CUNY). I consider how teachers and students described genres and how genres were assigned, written, and evaluated in specific situations. I conclude that genre is not a recipe for writing we can effectively list on the assignment sheet: instead, because it is a social practice, readers and writers make everyday genres interactively. Across unique situations, writers grapple with how to take an appropriate stance on material they must present as evidence to expert readers. Clearly, the complaints heard about students' writing show that it is not enough to describe requirements on a prompt. Because a prompt embodies a social practice, we would not *give* assignments as much as we would try to *enact* them in our classes. Ideally, we would provide our students with access to a situation where they could interact with readers and be exposed to their expectations in some way. Throughout this book, I cite the work of doctoral students and professors who, across the curriculum, did consider their assignments from this dynamic rhetorical perspective.

Genre study persuades us to consider related questions about the nature of rhetorical situations and the nature of expertise in writing. From genre study, we inquire what constitutes a situation, the extent to which writing expertise stretches across situations, and how we think people acquire expertise in more than one situation. Though it is not always apparent, this cluster of major questions frequently motivates debates about writing instruction that routinely occur in WAC faculty workshops on a campus. And as a result of the attention paid to genre, composition scholars are studying these questions more formally. Briefly, then, I consider them here as a foundation for the particular study of genre offered in subsequent chapters.

Genre study critiques the assumption that writing exists independently of its situation and that we could overtly teach forms like the college essay so students can smoothly apply them across situations. This is why scholars who draw from genre studies dispute the extent to which writing can be taught effectively in a composition course—or even in school at all (Beaufort; Freedman, and Adam; Smit; Waldo; Wardle, "'Mutt Genres'"). Others use genre theory to propose new and powerful first-year curricula in which students write genres defined by actual situations of use in community-learning contexts (Feldman) or in the disciplinary contexts of writing studies (Downs and Wardle). These new curricula insist that genres evolve from the specific situations where writers accomplish authentic tasks for readers. Without participating in, being immersed by the rhetorical situation, it is argued, writers do not acquire genres because they do not perform consequential rhetorical actions.

For this reason, some theorists define situation so narrowly it occurs only in the immediate context of its use. This is the case for Paul Prior, who studies the unique, fine-grained microhistory of literate acts unfolding at one moment in time. An everyday genre evolves from a situation formed by local or immediate expectations: one course, one semester, one professor. But, in this book, the level of analysis is not so fine-grained because I assume the situation may also be more or less shaped by the expectations of groups beyond the moment at a more abstract level: the institutional, discipline, or workplace. In public-health classes, teachers often assign community-mapping projects that are aligned with how the discipline imagines these genres perform social actions on the job; a mathematical proof is tightly aligned with the forms experts in this discipline almost exclusively write; a research essay in an introductory history class is aligned with the field, but its motives and therefore some of its conventions are shared among departments in the humanities. Each of the forms, in my experience, is also shaped by a teacher's particular motives in a given semester. Genre study allows us to consider this complexity of ordinary rhetorical situations in the university and to contemplate the interplay between immediate and more distant expectations.

How we define the rhetorical situation is also shaped by the degree to which we imagine writing is a general or more specialized ability; how we imagine the extent of that ability is, in turn, shaped by how we think people gain expertise in writing. If writing is a general ability, then once we learn to write, we can cross between and anticipate future situations. David Smit argues persuasively that composition studies has never adequately defined *writing ability* or proven that it is a general ability transferable across situations. If genre is a recurring response to a rhetorical situation, then we know genres cannot be fully acquired or taught outside their situation. Therefore, a novice cannot really learn to write a new genre without participating in the life of the social groups who make genres possible in the first place. If writing ability is local, we acquire and use it exclusively in the actual rhetorical situations where we are immersed.

Genre study highlights this tension between how we define writing ability—as a singular skill taught in first-year composition or as plural skills acquired in contexts of their use. Researchers like Aviva Freedman and Mark Waldo use situated literacy theory to analyze their data and to conclude, broadly, that writers acquire genres as they acquire the language and content typical of a field. According to the linguist James Paul Gee, the rhetorical practice a genre embodies can never be mastered through sheer learning, which he defines as overt instruction most commonly found in school; a language form like a genre must be acquired to a certain extent in the natural contexts of its use. In his widely cited theory, he proposes we master discourses, a more expansive concept than genres, by being immersed, first, in rich social contexts that prepare us to acquire specific genres later on. Gee asserts we master discourses through "enculturation (apprenticeship) into social practices through scaffolded and supported interaction with people who have already mastered the Discourse" (139).

The apprenticeship model of enculturation helps to explain how university experts acquire their genre knowledge and why it is not always accessible to us when we craft prompts and evaluate student papers. For instance, in composition studies, we have long resisted regarding the "personal essay" as a genre with a dense history and conventional features; this genre is assumed to grow out of the writer's, not the reader's, motives. But close study of how English teachers actually evaluate this genre reveals they bring distinct generic expectations to their reading (Broad; Feldman; Murray). As many researchers observe, experts gain their genre knowledge as the result of long apprenticeship, and often their field's rhetoric and how their expectations have been formed are not apparent to them (Currie; Geller; Giltrow and Valiquette). Moreover, across fields, some professors subscribe to an apprenticeship theory of genre knowledge: they acquired rhetoric through trial and error and expect their students will, too, without overt instruction (Strachan).

In sum, genre study asks us to reflect on how we define rhetorical situations, whether we think writers can cross between them, and how they acquire the knowledge to do so successfully (or not). One of the most compelling research questions in recent years has emerged from these questions raised by genre studies: why, after leaving the situation of the first-year writing course, do students seem unable to apply composition skills to new situations in general education or the disciplines? In the view of some genre theorists and supported by their empirical research, students cannot cross easily (or at all) between situations because learners do not learn to write by applying general strategies to specific situations but must acquire genres by participating in the situations from which these strategies originate. Especially for those influenced by the New Rhetoric, a guiding principle is that if we learn the content and language of a field, we'll acquire its rhetoric, too (Dias, Freedman, Medway, and Paré; Johns, *Genre in the Classroom* 8–10).

Despite its explanatory power, though, this view of how students acquire genre can be limited if it defines the term *situation* so narrowly it excludes a writer's possible movement between contexts. So far, the theory does not, for instance, explain how some students do move successfully between situations. I have observed proficient student writers consistently earn the high regard of readers across general-education courses; in my own program, I have found some evidence that a successful writer applies general strategy to new situations ("Mapping"). Nor does this view of literacy explain why, if students acquire genres only through immersion, this process appears insufficient to their teachers, who continue to join WAC programs hoping to improve their students' grasp of disciplinary genres.

Indeed, some recent research suggests there are many reasons for the widespread perceived lack of transfer of writing skills, one of which may be the consistently impoverished opportunity for students to practice across fields the rhetorical skills they learn in a composition course. Wardle suggests this may be the case with revision, a skill students in her longitudinal study said they learned in composition but did not have the opportunity to use in their major courses ("Understanding 'Transfer' from FYC"). Some students may themselves define *situation* so narrowly they believe composition skills are irrelevant outside the first-year course and do not apply across fields (Bergmann and Zepernick; McCarthy). We know, too, that one mark of expertise may lie in how experts adapt general strategies to meet the demands of particular situations. Reviewing research in cognitive science, David Kaufer and Richard Young argue that experts appear to use general strategies to solve specific problems, and they cite for support, among others, Donald Schon's classic studies of expertise. Possibly, one general strategy that proficient student writers use in school resembles the reflective capacity experts in Schon's study used to assess and then solve specific problems in their fields. It can be argued that neither writing teachers nor faculty in the disciplines have focused on teaching students to develop this reflective capacity (Nelms and Dively).

It is, finally, excessive to claim that global forces never affect local situations: even on a desert island, Deborah Brandt and Katie Clinton maintain, globalizing rhetoric leaves some unmistakable traces. As any WAC director quickly learns, the disciplines are never islands, either; various social groups composing the disciplines and their preferred genres share multiple points of contact across situations (Belcher; Journet; Thaiss and Zawacki, "How Portfolios" and *Engaged Writers*). One of the pleasures and challenges for WAC is to discover those moments when genre knowledge is shared across situation.

Thus, for these reasons, I define *situation* more broadly to include the expectations of both immediate and more distant social groups. I assume writers do (or could) apply some general strategies to local situations, and I suggest in chapter 3 that overt instruction can be useful provided it is connected to or aligned closely with specific rhetorical motives. This assumption implies that most situations are not narrowly defined and that writing ability may extend and thus be taught overtly to a certain extent across contexts. Further, I suggest the rhetorical expertise we claim in composition can be shared across situations with our colleagues. In the WAC program I describe, we assumed we could collaborate with professors to apply general rhetorical principles to local assignments, though, unlike programs where WAC specialists interact with faculty in workshops, we participated to a certain extent in the rhetorical situation, the classroom where genres were taught. Shared expertise, I suggest, can occur in some situations because a rhetorical situation exceeds one moment or place in time: it is composed of both local and more global expectations.

The focus on genre allows WAC specialists to study more deeply than we have what typicality, how individual writers manage the interplay between the local and the global expectations of readers, looks like in the university. But I am also interested in how we can introduce students to that interplay. In chapter 2, I approach typicality by focusing on rhetorical stance in three different situations and suggest through these examples that students may have a better chance of fulfilling their readers' expectations if the students participate in the situation in some way. By participation, I mean either that students respond to well-defined communicative situations or that they have the opportunity to practice rhetorical skills in ways that approximate how we know experts acquire genres. Through participation, I argue, students are better able to find an appropriate stance and turn information into something that counts as evidence for their readers.

As well, I suggest, in these examples and many others, that the professors who taught these courses clarified their goals and then aligned their prompts with those goals by conversing with someone from the WAC program, in our case a doctoral student (I explain the role of these students, the writing fellows, later on). With others, experts sharpen their expectations and clarify their tacit knowledge. In the best situations, experts might expand their expectations using rhetorical terms they had not encountered or thought to use before (see Geller). For instance, in the biology class referenced in chapter 3, the professor did not tell students to write the methods section of a lab report in a narrative mode because he had not realized the students did not know this. But, through peer review and talking with the fellows, he learned what students did not know, and they gained a better sense of his expectations for a standard lab report.

The discovery of rhetorical motive and how motive shapes a genre's conventions can be best achieved through the sort of dynamic social interchange exemplified by holding peer-review sessions, discussing models and graded papers, or consulting with colleagues and outsiders. This is probably why, in the program described, professors said on a survey that the WAC program's most valuable feature was conversing with the fellows. If genre does serve as a socializing force in our fields, it makes sense that even experts benefit from considering what written forms do in situations the writers find socially meaningful. The current volume gives examples of assignments that reflect how the doctoral students spent time in classrooms and from observation and conversation with experts adapted general rhetorical strategies to local settings.

The extent to which we can successfully adapt our tools, strategies, or principles across situations requires, of course, that rhetoricians consider how this adaptation occurs exactly. Kaufer and Young conclude that the model of expertise informing their early work with a scientist resembles what others similarly identify as the missionary or conversion approach where rhetoricians "bring" their knowledge to faculty in the disciplines so they can change their teaching (e.g., Jones and Comprone; Segal, Paré, Brent, and Vipond; Walvoord, Hunt, Dowling, and McMahon). By contrast, in the second model Kaufer and Young describe, WAC specialists do not share their expertise as much as they use it to become intense observers of rhetorical cultures or, as Judy Segal and her colleagues put it, anthropologists, describing how genres work in the contexts of their use. In this case, composition studies could not play an expansive role beyond documenting what occurs in particular situations.

But genre studies offers an interactive approach consonant with the third model Kaufer and Young propose. In their view, faculty can share their expertise with rhetoricians, and vice versa, to create new, possibly interdisciplinary, knowledge. Similarly, throughout, I offer examples of assignments that resulted from sustained discussion between experts in different fields; the appendixes provide a sampling of exercises from these partnerships. Such examples come from my work with faculty, tutors, undergraduates, and the writing-fellow doctoral students in the WAC program I directed at City College for seven years.

Chapter 1, "Sharing Genre Expertise," gives an account of how the fellows worked with City College faculty to implement the WAC program. What is always a complex endeavor was perhaps intensified in our case because the fellows, outsiders to the local campus culture whose contracts were set by a central authority, occupied ill-defined roles. Through careful observation of our interaction with faculty, we worked to define the fellows' roles. This involved giving fellows time to study, even participate in, the situation and with the faculty consider how to apply basic rhetorical principles to these situations. The faculty usually identified problems with assignments in their courses, and, after observing the context, the fellows offered them tools or activities informed by composition scholarship, such as the sequencing of complex skills or the segmenting of assignments to include invention activities. The fellows attempted to provide students with access to genres by creating situations allowing them to practice, to varying degrees, the typical habits experts have developed as a result of their apprenticeship in social groups.

The guiding research question in this program was always a practical one: based on what we learned in our partnerships, what good assignments and supports for assignments can we recommend to faculty? To answer that question, I asked two others:

How do students across disciplines talk about the relationship between writing and learning course content?
How do teachers across disciplines talk about and evaluate student writing?

Our program was based on a changing labor pool of doctoral students with varying research interests and backgrounds who worked with new faculty each semester. Therefore, our methods for studying these questions were multiple, ranging from naturalistic teacher research to formal evaluations of student writing. Chapter 1 also describes the research on student perceptions' of their learning and teachers' evaluation of student writing, two bodies of literature that shaped my questions, the methods we used, and the interpretations I draw from our studies of writing across the curriculum. My interpretation of evidence is further framed by genre theory and research. From this perspective, I try to answer the original question: what is a good assignment? I conclude that because genre is a social practice, an assignment must be aligned with the larger social motives the genre performs for readers in the first place.

Chapter 2, "Stance in Genre," considers how writers achieve authority to speak about evidence in university genres, a struggle, Bakhtin says, that lies at the core of the successful acquisition of all writing. Although in perception and longitudinal research, students frequently identify this struggle, the scholarship has not addressed stance as a central problem in writing genres. But at City College and many other institutions, students describe the problem they have ascertaining their involvement in formal genres and reconciling their personal motives as writers with the teacher's motives for writing. In composition and other general-education courses (e.g., Bergmann and Zepernick; Durst; Hunt; Nelms and Dively; Russell and Yañez; Wardle, "Understanding 'Transfer' from FYC") or in the major disciplines (Ariail and Smith; Carroll; Chiseri-Strater; Leki, "Living through College Literacy"; Herrington and Curtis; Marsella, Hilgers, and McLaren; Thomas, Bevins, and Crawford), researchers document how some students perceive difficulty finding a stance in impersonal genres, struggle over distinguishing fact from opinion, or simply resist taking the critical perspective on material their teachers request.

In this context, I consider that an assignment evolves from a situation informed by more than a single prompt. I examine how students' writing in three situations was framed by *teacher talk*— prompts, guidelines, warnings in class, commentary on papers. This teacher talk is equivalent, Janet Giltrow argues, to a university metagenre that students are aware of when they compose ("Meta-Genre"). Drawing, too, on recent linguistic study of authorial stance, I explore how the students express their presence, make judgments, select material, and align themselves with both readers and their evidence. In this regard, I am also examining what constitutes a typical stance in these university situations. Drawing on interviews, I claim the proficient students fulfilled their readers' expectations by using what Bakhtin calls typical evaluative phrasing, a blend of their own words with another's. In his view, a novice acquires this speech by assimilating another's words and not copying them, achieving the distinction between imitation and typicality. I conclude the students are more likely to achieve this typical authoritative speech when they can participate in the rhetorical situation in some meaningful way.

Here, I contrast the genres assigned in a graduate class and in a music-appreciation class with college essays assigned in a first-year psychology course. I distinguish between the stance students achieve in well-defined situations that offer participation and the struggles weaker writers may experience if they lack the opportunity to practice rhetorical skills. I speculate, too, that one difference among these genres lies in the extent to which they are, to adapt Paul Prior's phrasing, domesticated or wild; the college essay I consider is the fainter, domesticated shadow of a wilder case-study essay. One consequence of domesticating a wild genre is that the teacher talk surrounding the assignment appeared contradictory, and this may have hindered some students trying to find an appropriate stance. Therefore, besides urging faculty to consider the actual behavior of genres in the wild when they craft their prompts, I also suggest students endow university genres with more intense meaning when they can inhabit wilder roles. By trying on the expert's role, they may more clearly understand the particular social actions genres perform.

Especially in school, writers like some of those cited in this chapter lean on commonsense knowledge (their "opinions") also because they may not have much to say about a topic in the first place. Though not addressed as a central problem in the study of classroom genres, I assume invention's importance based partly on seventeen years of working with students at City College, whose texts are sometimes marked by brevity. But I also believe it is common for writing-intensive courses to exclude invention, which of course makes it all the more difficult for students to do more than state the facts, as Jennie Ariail and Thomas G. Smith found with a nursing student struggling to develop an appropriate stance in her writing. Based on their analysis of assignments in a college of nursing, they conclude, "In classical rhetorical terms, [the professors' guidelines] sacrifice invention at the altar of arrangement and style" (258).

In their powerful account of learning, Jean Lave and Etienne Wenger claim we find something to say to someone for some reason through sustained social interaction. Chapter 3, "Content in Genre," uses their theory to consider how writers find ideas and facts and, because having plenty of information is not enough, how they turn their material into evidence for readers. I contrast what researchers know about writing genre in the workplace with the standard teaching of genre across the curriculum, illustrating the arts of invention through an example from an architectural-history class.

In academic situations, finding good ideas is not enough since it is readers who ultimately decide which ideas are worthy of their attention. Typically, writers shape information into evidence by drawing distinctions: between common and expert knowledge; general statements and telling details; data and interpretation. Especially for writers who lack practice and confidence, it is difficult to ascertain the proper detail required by, for instance, a thesis statement, if they do not know anything about the readers whom they address. Knowing what readers expect is one way to grasp the social actions genres perform. To learn what readers want to know is essentially social knowledge requiring interaction with particular readers and exposure to genre expectations through talk, writing, and reading about models or drafts. I investigate these claims through examples from classes in biology, media communications, and art.

The power of the apprenticeship model that genre study brings to WAC lies in just this insistence: to learn a practice, we have to be immersed in social situations that provide steady contact with an audience. But, Lave and Wenger (and their adherents) seem also to insist, learning occurs implicitly, as a result of the immersion in the social context that gives meaning to the practice. Research on how students transfer writing knowledge between situations is not large, but what is available suggests that metacognition may, also, be a necessary aspect of apprenticeship that theorists have not fully addressed in the context of writing-intensive courses (Beaufort; Greene, "Question of Authenticity"). I argue for a more reflective view of apprenticeship models in which what matters is less a distinction between implicit and overt instruction and more how we can contextualize the genre in a class (Carter, Ferzli, and Wiebe). Chapter 3 ends by showing how a professor in anthropology and a fellow built an effective social context, explicitly aligning the prompts with the content, course goals, and rhetoric of the field.

The relationships between readers and writers define a genre, and when these relationships are new ones, even the most accomplished writers struggle to create unknown social roles. Professionals are perplexed when they encounter unfamiliar genres in part because they are exploring new subject matter, trying on new roles, and meeting unknown audiences. Experts find, for instance, that they are cast in the role of novice, and the experience is distressing (see Waldo 19). The economists whose writing Graham Smart studied had, he argues, to "reinvent their expertise" when they encountered a foreign genre in their workplace. Proficient student writers report similar disorienting experiences when they change major fields of study (Beaufort; Berkenkotter and Huckin) or cross from their majors, where they are gaining expertise, to general-education courses, where they encounter strange methodologies and assumptions about the world (Lane).

But some professors in the academy believe their students will solve the problem of transferring writing skills across situations by "picking up" genres on their own, without instruction, because this is the way they learned to write. From this perspective (shared, I indicated earlier, by some theories of situated literacy), a writer learns a genre by acquiring the field's special language, without deliberate instruction. In the conclusion, I challenge this widely appealing but ultimately limited view of learning. If we do not examine this version of the apprenticeship model that still holds tacit sway in our institutions, we may block students' access to genres.

Gee argues that apprenticeship must precede explicit instruction if we expect genuine language learning to occur: "If you have no access to the social practice, you don't get in the Discourse—you don't have it" (139). As he and other apprenticeship theorists note, schools are limited in how much access they can really give to the social practices privileged students have been immersed in long before they come to college. Since the 1970s, however, CUNY has challenged this view in its effort to provide a quality education to a working-class urban population. A study of writing and difference lies outside the scope of my inquiry, but cultural diversity formed the rhetorical situation of every class I cite, and it played a major role in professors' decisions to explore WAC.

Therefore, it is necessary to say that in 2000, City College was one of the most diverse four-year schools in the nation, with most students (at least 85 percent) falling into one or more of the categories federal granting agencies deem "nontraditional." While the students are nontraditional in terms of social class, race, ethnicity, age, country of origin, generation in their family to attend college, and life situation (they commute long distances, raise children without spouses, and work full-time), their linguistic diversity is, especially for their teachers, strikingly complex. Perhaps two-thirds of the students enrolled in any of the general-education courses where fellows worked spoke English as a second (or third) language or learned standard English as a second dialect. The case of an anthropology class in chapter 3 is common: of fifty students enrolled in two sections, the fellow reported they spoke twenty-three different languages.

Most professors and writing fellows in our WAC program were genuinely committed to teaching in this urban situation, and in whatever ever way they could, they hoped to offer students access to the social languages Gee describes. Institutions, I conclude, play a primary role here since improving writing instruction cannot be broadly effective if it remains a purely individual decision. This is one implication, too, of emerging research on the transfer of writing skills across university situations. The professors whose work I cite did not believe all their students would "pick up" genres. In the context of university support, they took explicit responsibility for widening their students' access to genres and enriching their university experience. Their commitment, supported by the university, to provide CCNY students with more access to powerful university genres, makes possible the discussion I offer in the following chapters.

# 1

## Sharing Genre Expertise

USUALLY, A FORMAL WAC PROGRAM begins with conversations between professors trained in English studies and professors from across the disciplines. The literature describes various relationships: WAC faculty come together to renew their teaching and consult with their peers on projects or, to fulfill a campus requirement, to attend workshops and seminars (e.g., Kipling and Murphy; Monroe; Segall and Smart; Thaiss, *Writing to Learn*; Walvoord, Hunt, Dowling, and McMahon; Young and Fulwiler). Sometimes, tutors offer substantial support through writing-fellow programs in which they play a wide range of roles (Soven, "Curriculum-based"). But no matter how WAC is defined on a campus, any serious effort will raise questions—sometimes, among WAC directors, it is a difficult debate—of who has the professional authority to teach writing (Kirscht, Levine, and Reiff). Because of its special interest in the relationship of writing to situation, genre studies presses those of us with expertise in composition to ask yet again: how do we share what we know effectively across situations?

The City College writing-fellow program was defined by one-to-one partnerships between the fellows and the faculty who chose to work with them for their own reasons, since there was no campus pressure to fulfill a writing requirement. Generally, faculty wanted to improve their teaching, often in the context of an urban campus serving students with complicated linguistic backgrounds; more particularly, they requested fellows because they wanted to revise and support their assignments. The fellows helped them to reconsider assignments in the context of their expertise in WAC: in the best partnerships, they could apply rhetorical principles to local situations. To do this well required they become familiar with some basic rhetorical principles and that they become familiar with the situation. Gaining this expertise—in composition, in the situation—was complicated because fellows brought such various backgrounds to the campus; they were trained in several disciplines, not just English studies, and they were outsiders to the campus culture.

But, by focusing on the relationship between rhetoric and situation, we did figure out how to define their roles on campus, and many fellows gained enough expertise, as I will describe, to help professors achieve their goals. This was primarily a teaching program dependent on new cohorts of fellows passing through it each year, dedicated in particular to answering the question, what makes a good assignment? Consequently, we devised a range of research methods to document our work, and this chapter concludes by describing my research questions and the multiple sources from which I draw examples.

## THE CUNY-WIDE WAC MANDATE

After moving to open admissions in the 1970s, CUNY endured steadily escalating attacks on its standards. Some of these attacks focused on writing instruction, and by the early 1990s, remedial courses became the focal point for withering critiques by local journalists and politicians. In response, CUNY took action to restore public faith in its municipal system and to garner better press from local outlets like the *New York Times* and *New York Post*. To upgrade standards for students, CUNY stiffened admissions requirements on some campuses, mandated a rising junior exam to test students' proficiency in college literacy, and created an Honors College. At the same time, to upgrade standards among faculty, the university increased research requirements and designated flagship programs and campuses. In this context, the Board of Trustees abolished remediation in writing and math at four-year colleges and in January 1999 voted on a resolution called "The Enhancement of Student Writing Skills." In brief, the board mandated that all seventeen colleges, including the law school, create WAC programs; the board also pledged university support through the CUNY writing-fellows program, which was to use "specially trained CUNY doctoral students who will assist in the delivery of intensive writing instruction" ("City University," 25).

A university-wide task force fleshed out the board's mandate by developing some guidelines for WAC that later were incorporated into CUNY's master plan for 2000–2005. In its report, the task force lists the hallmarks of successful programs, such as faculty development, and overviews the common features of writing-intensive courses nationwide (Iconis). Still, neither this task force nor the trustees mandated writing-intensive courses for CUNY-wide WAC; and neither the task force nor the board defined what exactly fellows would do on a campus, beyond establishing broad parameters for their labor.

The board's resolution gave each campus a cohort of fellows and funds to pay for release time from teaching for a campus WAC director and for faculty-development efforts. Many WAC directors came from their campus composition programs (as I did), and all were required to serve together on a university-wide committee, chaired by a university dean. In the fall of 1999, each campus received six writing fellows, whose contracts were negotiated by CUNY's Academic Affairs, the CUNY Graduate Center, and the faculty union. According to this contract, students who had completed their PhD coursework were eligible to work for two years as fellows during the academic semesters. Each fellow owed fifteen hours a week to campuses, and although they were not required to take a course, they were obligated to attend professional-development workshops sponsored by Academic Affairs throughout the year. Perhaps most important, CUNY fellows were mandated to help implement WAC programs and were prohibited from acting exclusively as tutors or graders.

Academic Affairs sponsored monthly meetings of the university-wide WAC committee, where the WAC directors vigorously debated the role fellows could play. One issue concerned the extent to which the program existed to educate fellows as future teachers. Another concerned the mandate requiring fellows to help faculty implement WAC programs on campus rather than tutor or work as graders. In this regard, WAC directors debated fellows' roles in the context of their expertise (or lack of it). How could graduate students mostly untrained in composition and some inexperienced as teachers work with faculty across the disciplines? Because they study at a campus in midtown Manhattan, the CUNY Graduate Center, the fellows were outsiders to local campus cultures spread across the city. Fellows list their top three choices of campuses on an application form, but often they are sent to campuses they do not choose in the outer boroughs of New York City with which they are largely unfamiliar. Given this circumstance, how would they implement programs if they did not know the students on a campus, especially given the bewildering diversity of institutional missions and CUNY undergraduates? Should fellows be assigned to faculty, courses, or departments? Should they be matched by discipline with faculty? How could Academic Affairs train fellows when their roles differed by campus? As described below, these questions were relevant for the fellows who came to City College.

### MODELS OF EXPERTISE

When they arrived on the City College campus in the early fall of 1999, four of the six new writing fellows lacked expertise in teaching composition. Only one was familiar with the campus, and all were exposed to WAC largely through a summer institute at the Graduate Center. Since we had no WAC program, they were assigned to a deputy provost, who in turn hired a literature professor from English to supervise them. The deputy provost also decided to assign them to partner with faculty she knew from her work as the director of the campus Center for Teaching and Learning.

Right from the start, the fellows experienced difficulty because neither they nor the faculty had developed a model of expertise that allowed them to effectively share their knowledge. In the fall of 1999, when they landed on our campus, the fellows assumed (and here I draw from an unpublished essay three of them later wrote) that City College faculty probably did not use writing as a way of learning but chiefly to evaluate their students and to record facts from textbooks. Fresh from their WAC workshop, they brought a conversion model of WAC to the campus, certain that they could give to faculty their particular expertise in writing. Some City College professors assumed the Graduate Center was providing them with tutors or graders. When some discovered this was not the case, one rumor circulated widely on campus that the program was only meant to provide financial aid for doctoral students. In the meantime, the fellows were assigned to work with particular professors who, uncertain of the fellows' roles, dismissed, sometimes abruptly, their attempts to build partnerships.

As more professors expressed disdain for both WAC and the fellows, the deputy provost turned to the chair of the English department for help. He recommended she hire me based on the experience I had directing the campus Writing Center and coordinating our well-known basic-writing program. Though I had given workshops to teachers in the humanities, my knowledge of WAC was limited, so I spent that semester reading with fellows in study groups, listening to faculty who came to the Center for Teaching and Learning, and attending university-wide WAC meetings. I assumed responsibility for the program during the following semester.

In the fall of 1999, the deputy provost assigned fellows to a biology lab, where they worked with professors for two years; the following spring, when I began the study group, they were paired with an art professor. These partnerships in biology and art, referred to in chapter 3, helped the fellows to discover a productive role. The fellows recalled how they began attending biology labs without a particular goal in mind, listened to lectures and took notes, and one day thought that peer review might work to help students produce better lab reports. When they approached one of the course professors with this idea, she was positive, and the fellows reported they experienced, for the first time, a sense of success in one of their assigned courses. Possibly, as one of these professors commented to me later on, biology was especially receptive to the fellows at this moment in time because the department had begun to reconsider its entire undergraduate curriculum, including the role that writing plays in science education.

While the fellows worked in biology, the deputy provost and I considered how to define their roles more officially at City College. To this conversation, I brought experience with an ethnographic study of how English teachers worked with peer tutors who were as-signed to help them in their classrooms ("Shifting Roles"). I learned from that study that some English teachers were uncomfortable working closely with outsiders who either challenged their exper-tise or required too much time to collaborate with (or both). We subsequently ended the practice of assigning tutors to teachers in our writing program and, instead, spent time defining the fellows' roles in advance for the teachers who elected to work with them for their own reasons.

As we considered the English teachers' relationships to tutors, the deputy provost and I began to observe closely to see what did work in successful interactions that semester between fellows and faculty from economics, psychology, and education. By the end of the fall semester 2000, we ended the practice of assigning fellows to faculty, and we created an application I sent across campus, in-viting professors to join our program for reasons they identified. We set broad parameters that we refined in subsequent semesters: in exchange for a small stipend and a fellow's time, faculty had to consult directly with fellows on a project and then produce an artifact to share with professors in a public forum (e.g., workshops or our handbook and the like).

The application asked faculty to describe their courses' roles in their departments and learning objectives and to indicate the proj-ect they wanted to work on with a fellow. Some faculty defined their objectives quite broadly; a professor of anthropology wrote on her application, "I want to improve my students' writing." Others, however, identified particular assignments they wanted to revise or tools they needed to support their assignments. For instance, when a professor of architectural history applied for a fellow, she said she wanted to develop a sketchbook assignment. In 2005, professors who responded to a survey ranked "clarifying and developing assign-ments" as the second most valuable aspect of the program ("Talking to the fellows" was the first).

By the spring of 2001, the fellows thought they understood how faculty and writing specialists productively share their expertise. From the close observation of classroom cultures they conducted in fall 2000, they discovered, for instance, that faculty assigned writing for many reasons and were passionate about improving their students' work. From these encounters, the fellows said they realized they had not only to immerse themselves in the rhetorical situation a class represents but also to become, to some extent, participants in it. Describing their work with faculty, WAC scholars identified a similar moment when rhetoricians venturing out of their own fields into others shifted their roles: from the missionary to the anthropological to the participatory or interactive role (Segal, Paré, Brent, and Vipond; Walvoord, Hunt, Dowling, and McMahon). Kaufer and Young speculate, however, that the fruitful exchange works both ways: a rhetorician enlarges a scientist's view of writing, but the scientist, in turn, enlarges the rhetorician's. They conclude, "Neither the writing teacher nor the content teacher can select the role of anthropologist or native. Both must play both roles. Both must be willing to travel" (102). The City College fellows also reported they moved from an observational role to become, in the most intense cases, coparticipants who interacted with experts in distinct rhetorical situations.

By the end of fall 2000, fellows had worked with enough partners that I drafted a list of what they did in different classes and included it with the application and related introductory materials I sent to faculty across campus. I updated this list over the semesters, eventually publishing it online. Figure 1 suggests how fellows played various roles in classrooms. In some cases, fellows gave workshops to students, usually on the APA documentation style, with minimal collaboration from the faculty. At the other end of the spectrum, faculty collaborated with fellows on developing entire course books and curricula, as when a philosophy professor and a fellow created a substantial book of reading exercises.

More typically, fellows worked with professors to revise and support their assignments. Revisions included clarifying the wording of prompts through conversation about the professors' goals, both for the assignment and the course. Sometimes, fellows would study graded papers, discuss these with professors, and make tools like a rubric to help professors focus their evaluation. Frequently, revision meant segmenting one major assignment or sequencing a series of shorter assignments across the semester. When professors chose to segment an assignment, they would assign multiple drafts or invention exercises to prepare students to write about course material in advance of the final project. In class, fellows gave workshops to students that supported these segmented assignments: peer review of drafts, planning exercises such as heuristics or double-entry notebooks, and annotation exercises. To help students find ideas, fellows developed invention assignments, or to gain a sense of a genre's typicality, they created modeling exercises. To give students the opportunity to practice rhetorical skills in ways approximating expert practice, fellows helped their professors segment assignments across the semester.

Finally, to add to the complexity, fellows shifted roles as they spent time with faculty in two or more courses offered in successive semesters. If faculty worked on the same course for two semesters with a fellow, the professors often spent time planning new as-

Preparation of course materials
- Research methods for teaching writing in a discipline/profession.
- Build reading and writing activities into a syllabus.
- Develop assignments and sequences of assignments.
- Creating writing-to-learn and informal reading/writing assignments.
- Facilitate the use of online-course environments for literacy.
- Develop course-specific writing handbooks/guidelines.

In-class support for students and faculty
- Model writing pedagogy by giving in-class workshops to students.
- Develop and facilitate the creation of student publications.
- Read papers and develop rubrics or guidelines for assessment/ grading.

Research, evaluation, and dissemination
- Participate in faculty workshops at CCNY and CUNY.
- Participate in assessment studies (e.g., conducting naturalistic research) to show what is or is not working.
- Develop materials for handbook, Web site, and/or video.

Fig. 1. Work that writing fellows did with faculty partners

signments in one semester and then implementing these the next semester, thus spending less direct time with their fellows, although there were exceptions to this pattern when professors requested, for instance, fellows to play a research rather than a pedagogical role in the second semester.

Thus, fellows played various roles in classes and experienced varying degrees of professional collaboration with numerous faculty at different points in the academic year. In the partnerships the fellows found most fulfilling, they enjoyed the intense collaboration the first group of fellows called *coparticipant roles*. Fellows played this role with all the professors whose work I cite in this book with the exception of the jumbo psychology class referenced in the next chapter.

One example of the coparticipant role suffices to illustrate how a professor shared genre expertise with fellows. In 2002, Rebecca Hatfield described her work with the fellows; the essay for her colleagues was published in our faculty handbook. Italics are added to highlight her comments referring to her overall goals and her interaction with fellows. She begins by describing her initial reasons for requesting a fellow:

> There are two challenges I have faced in teaching writing skills and in using writing to assess thinking skills and mastery of psychological content. *One challenge is how to integrate writing instruction into the psychology content without distracting unduly from the content that needs to be covered in a semester.* A second challenge is how to provide feedback on writing that is manageable for me and meaningful for the students. A related issue is how to provide feedback so that students that improve their writing can notice and appreciate this improvement.

Hatfield later explains how she worked with fellows and what goals they achieved:

> Early in the semester I contacted the Writing Fellows Project at City College and had the good fortune to be invited by the Director to come and meet with the Fellows and discuss ways that they might assist me. *After a series of very brief meetings, and several visits by the Fellows to my classroom as observers,*

which the Fellows conducted with efficiency, they produced a plan to help me teach writing to our Psychology majors in my Advanced Research Methods course. *We decided* that they would conduct a one-hour workshop on "assessing errors in your own writing" and on "the importance of rewriting drafts." *We also agreed* that they would produce some tools that would help me teach students about writing psychological reports and correct their writing samples. *The Fellows and I worked together.* However, the major work was primarily done by the Fellows to produce several products that I was able to use during the semester. These included (a) guidelines on how to write a literature review; (b) a peer assessment protocol; (c) a grading rubric for psychology research reports. *The Fellows interviewed me to find out what I wanted, what I knew and what would be helpful and then turned these interviews into tools that I could use. . . .*

What did I gain from all this? Firstly, a great respect for . . . the CCNY Writing Fellows. Secondly, very good feedback from my students this semester on how much they learned about their own writing and, from at least a handful, that they felt a sense of accomplishment and improvement in their writing. Thirdly, I gained some relief from the drudgery of reading 'term' papers. *I think the system the Fellows and I developed, with some refinement, will be an excellent tool that will carry me through helping students develop writing projects and giving them adequate feedback on them.* (Henriksen et al 26)

The fellows started with an anthropological role, talking to the professor and observing her classes and, over time, together developed various tools and exercises (not all described here) that they "agreed" would address her goals. By aligning the prompt with what was going on in class, they addressed the major challenge Hatfield identified: "to integrate writing instruction into the psychology content" (26). In this case, the partnership was productive because both parties appeared willing to travel across the lines of expertise.

## WRITING-FELLOW EXPERTISE

The CUNY WAC directors wondered how fellows could acquire enough expertise—in rhetoric, in a field, or on a campus—to help implement WAC programs. Hatfield's account illustrates how, on the City College campus at least, fellows were introduced to specific rhetorical situations. Typically, I invited applications, faculty set some broad objectives, usually focused around improving their assignments, and fellows based their preliminary meeting with faculty on the application; soon after, they began to study the rhetorical situation by attending class and reading course materials.

Each week, the fellows together also met with me so they could deepen their knowledge of composition studies and consider its relationship to the multiple situations they encountered. The program changed each year, but generally, the weekly sessions in the fall semester concerned basic rhetorical principles: segmenting large assignments or sequencing shorter ones, clarifying prompts by defining communicative situations, developing writing-to-learn and invention activities to support assignments. To illustrate these principles, I gave the fellows (and their professors) books like John Bean's *Engaging Ideas* or Katherine Gottschalk and Keith Hjortsoj's *Elements of Teaching Writing* and articles fellows identified as helpful on low-stakes writing (Elbow) or sequencing assignments (Kiniry and Strenski).

During these lively meetings, we grappled with the central issues involving the relationship between rhetoric and situation. For instance, one topic I discussed with several cohorts of fellows was whether, and how, to recommend the use of student or professional models to the faculty, many of whom raised interesting questions about the role that models play in learning to write. To what extent is discussing one model student paper helpful to a whole class? How can writers move from a general model to the specific version? What distinguishes imitation from the assimilation of forms? One conclusion we reached, early in the program, was that models were only useful if they were integrated into the rhetorical situation of the class and that a range of models was probably optimal.

I also tried to contextualize fellows' individual projects with a campus and disciplinary perspective. I gave different groups material about writing and learning at City College, such as excerpts from Marilyn Sternglass's *Time to Know Them* and essays about writing in the disciplines where we had partners. Though fellows usually combed the Internet to find their own resources, I often made specific essays available to them to fit a situation. If, for instance, a fellow was working in a history class, I would find a portfolio from a previous history class if we had one and an essay about teaching writing in history, such as John Breihan's thoughtful account (Walvoord with Breihan).

As important, some fellows learned to transfer rhetoric across situations, adapting what they learned from each other to new situations. One example of this process suffices: Julia Mitchell was trained in cultural anthropology, but she had no substantial teaching experience when she came to City College. Isabelle Hardy, a fellow from English, had experience teaching writing workshops, and she spent a semester with Mitchell in an upper-division seminar, where they gave workshops to students from many majors on a complex research assignment. Appendix 1 includes a reflective essay Mitchell wrote describing a peer-review session she conducted with a professor teaching introductory anthropology. In this essay, Mitchell mentions that she got the idea for the format she used in the anthropology class from her previous work in the seminar. The exercises I have included alongside Mitchell's illustrate how typical this cross-situational sharing was among the fellows.

The majority of new fellows acted as apprentices in the way Jean Lave and Etienne Wenger describe the role: they could, with a few exceptions, stay on the sidelines without being expected to lead a project during the first semester. New fellows were paired with veterans, and they spent their first semester on campus reading WAC literature and course portfolios, watching veterans give workshops, and listening while their more experienced peers interacted with faculty and developed materials to present during study groups. At the same time, fellows attended workshops at the Graduate Center, including presentations given by their peers from City College. In different years, they also learned about WAC by attending presentations several City College faculty gave at the Graduate Center or on campus.

Fellows did have some time to reflect on their growing expertise. The first cohort wrote detailed notes about their preliminary meetings with faculty, and they began to assemble portfolios of their work. The second cohort kept process notes, a genre introduced by Mitchell. By their second year, some had trouble sustaining these lengthy notes, so I discontinued the practice, particularly in light of an increase in faculty applications. While a few also presented their work at CUNY or 4Cs, mainly the fellows assessed their work through reports they wrote and materials they assembled to document their partnerships in course portfolios. This was the case, for instance, in biology classes, where, over several months, three fellows kept detailed notes describing peer-review sessions.

## DOCUMENTING SHARED EXPERTISE

I developed three major research questions to study our work in this program:

- How do students across disciplines talk about the relationship between writing and learning course content?
- How do teachers across disciplines talk about and evaluate student writing?
- By exploring these questions, what good assignments and supports for assignments could we recommend to faculty?

This was a flexible program that attempted to respond to the objectives faculty established. Further, because it depended on a transitory pool of fellows with various training in research methods, the sources of data I draw from are multiple. They include these:

- Formal studies approved by internal review board: two naturalistic studies and four holistic assessments of student writing
- Formal surveys of students (every semester) and two program surveys of faculty

- IRB-approved interviews with students in selected classes
- Program materials for handbook, film, and Web site that included interviews
- Fellows' reports on program data
- Teacher research organized into course portfolios for each partnership

Below, I briefly describe the research that frames my questions and how we gathered and organized material.

My interest in students' perceptions of how they learn was shaped by research conducted at City College by Mina Shaughnessy and by my colleague Marilyn Sternglass. I drew further understanding from a CUNY subcommittee I chaired on assessment and research, whose members gathered studies across campuses and gave two separate presentations at 4Cs on how students, faculty, and fellows perceived CUNY-wide WAC (e.g., Cripps, Stanley, Soliday, and Garretson). The central finding in this research reflects the national conclusion: students believe they learn more content in small classes where they frequently discuss, write, and revise and receive frequent feedback from readers (Beason and Darrow; Carroll; Hilgers, Bayer, Stitt-Bergh, and Taniguchi; Hilgers, Hussey, and Stitt-Bergh; Light; *National Survey of Student Engagement*).

In 2000, a fellow trained in composition studies and I worked together to develop a program survey focusing on whether a writing-intensive course affects students' perceptions of learning course content and their approach to writing assignments. Fellows gave surveys in classes of thirty or fewer students, although the fellows did not administer them to all their courses. We revised this survey two years later, and a fellow from sociology tabulated and analyzed the second instrument (459 responses in twenty-two classes). We asked students whether they thought writing helped them to learn course material and whether they improved as writers; whether they drafted their work after taking the course; and whether the course differed from others in terms of the quality of feedback they received, their grades, and the amount of writing assigned. In an open-ended question, we asked students to list supports for writing in the class they found useful.

Consistently, more than two-thirds of students we surveyed strongly agreed or agreed that compared to other courses they were taking, they received more feedback from professors, improved their writing, and learned course content more thoroughly in the writing-intensive course. Doing annotation exercises, receiving feedback from professors, and writing drafts were the supports students mentioned most often as helping them learn to write and learn course material. Like their peers nationwide, City College students reported they were more engaged with learning in writing-intensive courses. One could say, then, that this research provides one basis for claiming that students learn course material better when they write about it in socially dynamic situations.

To gain a more fine-grained picture, I asked fellows to interview students from classes, either on audiotape or video. I developed questions focusing on whether students found particular assignments easy or difficult and why; for each course, I listed the supports I knew had been used (such as annotation or drafting) and asked if any were helpful and why. The fellows had only limited time to interview students, so we selected certain classes where they and the professor had time to allow this study. The fellows solicited consent from volunteers and from 2002 to 2005 interviewed fifty-six students from a range of classes. Some of these students received a small stipend when I had the funds; because they were volunteers, they were never representative of the whole class. I transcribed the interviews with substantial help from an English major from the CUNY Honors College.

To explore the second research question, how faculty evaluate student writing, I focused on the language that faculty used to describe their assignments: warnings in class, formal guidelines or rules, prompts, graded papers, formal assessments, and interviews. The research on how faculty in other disciplines evaluate student writing comprises unrelated studies employing different methods, and it provides a conflicting picture on the question of the extent to which expert readers apply discipline-specific knowledge to student texts (Beason; Leki, "Good Writing"; Mallonee and Breihan; Smith; Soven, *What the Writing Tutor*; Thaiss and Zawacki, *Engaged Writers*, "How

Portfolios"). Moreover, most studies focus on one aspect of a teacher's preference, such as written commentary on papers. But in their separate studies, Janet Giltrow and Sharon Stockton assume that genre expectations exceed a graded paper since an expert's genre knowledge is largely tacit and involves more than one reader's response. Giltrow examines that knowledge in many sources, including interviews, prompts, and written commentary, and she concludes that what she calls *teacher talk* constitutes a metagenre of which students are aware when they compose their texts. Teacher talk about genres in the university establishes a powerful context for writing, a dynamic body of "wordings and activities, demonstrated precedents or sequestered expectations—atmospheres surrounding genres" ("Meta-Genre" 195). To examine "argument," Giltrow focuses on this word and its relationship to "collocates," the related words faculty used when they describe argument, such as thesis, evidence, and voice ("'Argument' as a Term"). Similarly, when I examine *stance* in the next chapter, I focus on the different words faculty and students use to describe their tacit sense of how writers address their readers about evidence.

One of my sources of teacher talk is the formal evaluation of student writing I conducted from 2003 to 2006 in four classes (180 finished papers in media communications, anthropology, music, and world humanities). With considerable help from an undergraduate assistant and a fellow trained in scientific research, I solicited students' consent, and then solicited readers from the departments and the CUNY Graduate Center. Consulting faculty and fellows, I developed rubrics and then conducted each reading using standard holistic methodology. In each case, I surveyed readers before they scored papers, asking them to define the purpose of the specific genre being assessed; after the scoring sessions, I interviewed the readers, again asking them to define the genre's purpose and whether the rubric they used adequately captured their generic expectations.

Another source for studying how teachers talk about writing is naturalistic classroom research, which also yields a rich glimpse into how students perceive the link between writing and learning course content. Course professors in early-childhood development and science of society invited us to conduct studies including interviews with them and their students, surveys designed for that class, and regular observations. But this method was too time consuming to sustain for fellows who were juggling several partners during one semester. Thus, a chief source for studying how students perceive their learning and teachers talk about genre comes from the fellows' teacher research, not approved by the IRB, contained in the seventy course portfolios they assembled to document their ongoing work with professors. The portfolios blend classroom observation and informal interviews with course documents, graded papers, transcripts of class discussions, and reflective reports.

To organize their diverse material, the first cohort of fellows created a checklist (see fig. 2). Typically, what fellows chose to include in course portfolios reflects several factors: the role they played in a class; their disciplinary training, which affected what they thought was important to include; and their commitment to the program or the time they had to assemble documents during the rush of finals' week. In cases where they enjoyed coparticipant roles, fellows documented *how they gained expertise in both rhetoric and the situation*

___ Number of students in the course
___ Faculty application
___ Articles
___ Course syllabus (and preexisting, if any)
___ Preexisting assignments (if any)
___ Writing fellow's one-page description of the course
___ Meeting reports
___ Correspondence with professor (e-mail and otherwise)
___ List of materials worked on for the course (both those implemented and not)
___ Student surveys and tabulations
___ Writing fellow's one-page description of impact on the course
___ Student papers
___ Other materials
Completed by:
Date:

Fig. 2. Writing-fellow portfolio checklist

(course readings they annotated, research on writing in the discipline, and planning notes), *their relationship to the professor* (e-mail correspondence, interview reports, drafts of exercises and prompts), and *their relationship to the students* (surveys, observational notes or tapes they made of classes). As readers who have used portfolio pedagogy would expect, this naturalistic methodology reflects the individual's perceptions of what happened in a class: the portfolios are not standardized, and thus they vary in quality and scope. But in the cases where fellows played coparticipant roles, the portfolios do provide a rich, unique glimpse of the everyday situations in which assignments were developed and evaluated.

I encouraged fellows to develop projects of their choice that would leave an institutional trace of their presence in the program. Some chose to develop materials we could use to publicize WAC, while others conducted their own qualitative studies or evaluated data we had collected in earlier semesters. The first two cohorts assembled a substantial handbook for faculty that included Hatfield's essay and examples of her classroom work. Brigid Kelly, who was trained in qualitative research methods, coded interviews from three classes and wrote a thoughtful report that sheds light on how students perceive the relationship between general rhetorical principles and particular writing assignments. Christina Ballantine, a fellow studying botany, spent two semesters interviewing faculty, fellows, and students for a fifteen-minute film we showed to audiences at CUNY and beyond, *Access to Learning*.

I use these various sources to consider students' perceptions of learning and teachers' expectations for their learning. But our attempts to document our work were always subordinate to the question, how can we define good practice? By the third year of directing this program, I could say to new fellows that an assignment is more likely to succeed if the professors can align it in some way with what they want students to learn in the course. I reframe this principle from the perspective of the social actions genres perform. If teachers can articulate the purpose given to a genre by the social group that awards it meaning in the first place, inexperienced writers will more fully grasp the conventions of the genre because they understand their readers' expectations. Sometimes, a motive becomes clear to the experts if they can interact with novice writers by allowing them to participate in a situation rather than write about it. By grasping motive, the inexperienced writers are in a better place to understand where they stand in relationship to evidence and to present something that counts as evidence for readers.

# 2

## Stance in Genre

FROM A RHETORICAL PERSPECTIVE, no content is free floating but must be governed by someone's angle of vision, or *stance*. Researchers assert that finding a stance poses problems for writers in new situations because, to become proficient, they are acquiring ways of seeing and believing typical of a field (Greene, "Making Sense"; Herrington, "Composing One's Self"; Lane). Stance requires writers do more than present information: they perceive and judge it in some way. To a certain extent, genres constrain writers' unique viewpoints since the generic stance reflects how others typically perceive content in similar circumstances. In the academy, readers highly value evidence, and so how writers relate to content plays perhaps a more distinct role for us than it does for readers of other genres.

To treat evidence properly, writers learn the distance they should maintain from readers and the typical words they should use to talk about evidence. Writers must, of course, understand the content in order to find an appropriate stance (an issue discussed in chapter 3). Here, the focus is on the subtle social knowledge writers need to speak confidently to readers, which is complicated when they encounter new and seemingly impersonal genres. In the latter, writers have to project their own presence while also respecting the presence of others.

Always, stance is appropriate in the context of the social action genres perform. In the university, motive includes what teachers think the genres they assign do in their disciplines or professions but also in their courses, programs, and institutions. To judge whether a student fulfills motive, teachers respond to the writer's presence in a text; the quality of this presence helps them decide whether a student has learned something in a course. Students align themselves with the material and with readers, but this is a complicated rhetorical stance for some students to manage if they struggle to figure out where they are involved in university genres. In particular, understanding the status of a writer's opinion is, university students report, a widespread difficulty, especially if a student is not sure what social action a genre performs.

To study stance, linguists analyze how speakers or authors use evaluative language. Bakhtin's analysis is especially relevant because he describes how a novice gradually learns to employ the words and phrases typical of a genre's evaluative language. His theory helps us to address the problem of typicality and to distinguish between the imitative and the generic. Similarly, I suggest successful student writers convince their teachers they've gained enough expertise by using typical speech, a blend of their own and another's words. In this regard, I contrast two genres (educational research essay and concert review) with the college essay in the context of teacher talk or the metagenre for the assignments. Judging, too, from what students wrote and from interviews, I speculate they are more successful when they have some access to the rhetorical practice typical of expert groups. One means of access occurs when they inhabit roles that they find, in some way, meaningful. I conclude that the college essay is a domesticated version of the wilder form and argue that if we can study genres in the wild, we can enrich how we teach the writer's stance in the everyday writing we assign.

#### DEFINING STANCE IN GENRES

In this chapter, I use the familiar rhetorical term *stance* to consider where authors stand in relation to readers and their material. *Stance* is difficult to define because, most broadly, it involves epistemology (seeing, being, or presence) and ideology (beliefs, commitments, or values). I use the word to indicate how writers express their presence and how they see and value their evidence. But teachers and students do not use the word *stance* to describe how writers present their evidence because the term is discipline specific. Instead, they use other words to describe a host of qualities that collocate with stance without being equivalent to it. For example, faculty used "position," "perspective," "point of view," "bias," "opinion," "focus," "engagement," and "voice" when they were describing the appropriateness of the writer's role in a text. For their part, students trying to talk about their involvement in university genres tended to use words like "bias," "opinion," "fact," and "voice."

It's unsurprising we would use multiple related terms, because, as Susan Hunston and Geoff Thompson argue in their study of authorial stance, linguists themselves use a range of terms and categories (see, for example, Christie and Martin's exhaustive list). To address the problem, Hunston and Thompson propose a "combining approach" to evaluative language. Evaluative language can be found, they say, in lexis, grammar, whole stretches of text (for example, a section called "implications" or "evaluation"), and in the selection of material (the "point of view" professors often mention). By analyzing evaluative language, Hunston and Thompson conclude, the linguist can identify the elusive "authorial stance." To examine stance in three genres, then, I focus on how students employ evaluative language. I consider how student writers use metadiscourse, identified by composition scholars as indicators of involvement, along with their lexis, grammar, and selection of material.

I also turn to Bakhtin to help explain a contradiction that arises when teachers talk about stance in student writing. As other researchers record (e.g., Giltrow, "Meta-Genre"; Lillis; Stockton; Strachan), professors sometimes give students conflicting advice concerning stance. We've all heard professors tell their students, for instance, to "use their own words," "give their opinions," and "take a position" and at the same time warn them "not to copy," "use formal language," "cite sources," and so on. At other times, as Elizabeth Wardle found in her study of a first-year writing program, professors advise students to write about specialized material to someone who knows nothing about it ("Mutt Genres"). These requests—made in class or during a conference, on a prompt, or in a formal guide for writing—may, as Janet Giltrow speculates, reflect a conflict at the heart of how academics feel about specialized genres. Bakhtin's theory of speech genres suggests, too, that the metagenre is confusing because acquiring an expert stance involves using both one's own and the other's words, a blending that is captured by the request to "use your own words" while referencing another's speech.

Bakhtin argues that the speaker's authority in relation to others lies at the heart of acquiring what he calls "speech genres." In his influential theory, he claims that while we all have unique experiences with language, our experiences with others shape the genres we use. Gradually, he explains, individuals internalize the words of other people and, with those words, the social worlds, ways of talking, being or knowing, and cultural values they represent. This sociolinguistic experience, he goes on to say, "can be characterized to some degree as the *process of assimilation*—more or less creative—of others' words" (89; emphasis added).

Assimilation involves finding a speech that is neither wholly native nor foreign but a mixing of words from two social worlds. Our "utterances" are "filled with others' words, varying degrees of otherness or varying degrees of 'our-own-ness,' varying degrees of awareness and detachment." In these terms, to successfully assimilate a foreign genre, writers have to creatively rework the other's speech into their own speech. To gain the authority to speak, writers incorporate alien words into their own expressions: "These words of others carry with them their own expression, their own evaluative tone, which we assimilate, rework, and re-accentuate" (Bakhtin 89).

Ultimately, Bakhtin stresses the creativity of stance, especially in impersonal genres where a writer has to find a speech that exists *between* authors and their sources: writers cannot copy other words but neither can they continue to speak their own native language. Writers must move between their own everyday speech and expert words to gradually assimilate not the exact but the *typical words* that sources use, signaling their involvement with the material. In this way, writers tell readers what they think is true about evidence and how they evaluate its worth. When, then, professors ask students to "take your own position" while also warning them not to display their "bias," they are describing a complex process of assimilation that their teacher talk, a metagenre in itself and an atmosphere surrounding university genres, does not sufficiently explain.

## STANCE IN THE RESEARCH-ESSAY GENRE

Vivian Allen, a professor in the School of Education, identified rhetorical stance as a key issue when she described her expectations for research writing in both undergraduate and graduate classes. Echoing several of her colleagues with whom we also worked, Allen said her students sometimes wrote *book reports*, not research papers. The difference, she explained, lies in the quality of perspective the writer exerts over the material.

In spring 2003, Allen worked with two fellows in an undergraduate course to revise her research assignment, which in education typically asks students to connect scholarship with their observations of children's behavior. For the undergraduate class, two fellows developed a rich portfolio of invention activities and segmented informal writing exercises to support this genre. In fall 2004, when Allen taught the same course, though this time to graduate students, she invited one of the fellows from the fall class to play a research, not a pedagogical, role. Since Allen and her colleagues gave similar assignments, we hoped this study might yield information useful to our many partners in the School of Education.

I interviewed Allen in the summer, after she had turned in her grades, and together we considered her comments on the papers students had written for both undergraduate and graduate courses. As she reflected on her teaching, Allen described how, she had noticed over the years, her students had trouble using the language typical of educational research and thus appropriately addressing their readers. In early-childhood-development class, which she taught to both undergraduates and graduate students, Allen had tried to solve the problem by experimenting with how she assigned and presented the course's chief genre, which her colleagues also used, a long paper requiring students to describe the research on a topic and then link that research to their observations of children's behavior. At first, she asked her students to read at least three articles and then link this research to their observations, but in response to this assignment, Allen recalled, "What I would get was three book reports, or three chapter reports or article reports. This person says this, this person says this, this person says this. Period. No introduction, no point of view, no conclusion, no nothing, just *this is this*." Allen addressed the problem by breaking the long research-paper assignment into two shorter, separate assignments. In the first one, a research essay, the students would "critically discuss" articles "in their own words"; in the second assignment, they would "observe," not interpret, children's behavior at school and then relate what they saw to a major developmental theory (see appendix 2). Despite the change in the assignment, however, some students still had problems with stance in the second research paper. Allen commented, "Some of them did a *response paper*, mostly a response, like, 'I agree with Erikson,' and I thought, that's all well and good, but that's not what this assignment is all about."

The next spring semester, when she worked with fellows, Allen again addressed the problem of stance in all her classes. She recalled she wrote a paragraph to illustrate the writer's proper degree of involvement with sources. She recalled how, during this class, she described to her students the writer's role in research essays: "I didn't want them to feel like once again, they weren't asked to put any of themselves in the paper, so I wrote this little paragraph . . . where I pointed out to them that they are involved, like their brains and their personal criticism are involved just in doing the synthesis, that they are somehow involved." Allen wanted the students to understand that the typical degree of closeness she privileges lies in "what you choose to focus on": "Their personal criticism is involved just in doing the synthesis." Quoting herself speaking in class, Allen summed up her expectations for students writing research essays: "I want to see if you can *explain someone else's theory in your own words* and that you can think about and articulate on paper how that relates to somebody else's ideas on the same topic. [I want the students to establish] the focus of this subject" (emphasis added). Allen's metagenre, her body of expectations, warnings, and advice, suggests that students need, in Bakhtin's terms, to assimilate, not imitate, the social language typical of educational research.

Allen justified this critical stance by linking it to her broader motives for assigning research essays in the first place. She judged her students' writing in the context of what she thought her assignments accomplished in a professional context (as did all the professors with whom we worked in the School of Education). In this class, the specific motive of the research paper she regularly assigns aims to shift how her students view the everyday problems they encounter in the schools. Allen hopes that by doing research, her students will view typical problems, such as children's aggression, from a research, not a commonsense, angle. Recalling her own experience as a teacher in a prestigious preschool, she said she hoped this exposure to research would empower early-childhood educators, occupying the most elementary rung of the educational ladder, when they interacted with parents and administrators. Allen did not expect her students to become researchers but to use insights from research in the workplace.

At midterms and finals, the fellow, Stasia Wilson, interviewed focal students from Allen's class about their reactions to the two major assignments (research and observing-a-child-at-school essays). An experienced preschool teacher whose first language is not English, Marcos Espinoza had earned a liberal-arts degree at another college and, two decades later, returned to City for his master's degree in education. Allen said that after revision, Espinoza produced final papers satisfying her expectations, and she indicated she was pleased with his progress.

In this class, Espinoza and his peers had access to a rich social discussion of genre, in part because Allen segmented both major assignments in several ways. For the first assignment, an essay where students had to "critically discuss" research articles "in their own words," she required students to read articles, post summaries on a course-management site, and to give a short presentation in class on their chosen topic. She also gave students a workshop in class on how to use the APA style. For the second essay, requiring students to apply developmental theory to their observations of children at school, Allen modified the observation exercise Wilson developed for the undergraduates so her graduate students could also practice, in class, taking nonjudgmental notes about children's behavior (see appendix 2). For both major assignments, Allen gave her students written and oral feedback on their summaries and drafts.

For the first research-essay assignment, Espinoza wrote a seven-page paper about separation anxiety, a topic he said he chose by listening to students' presentations in class. The excerpts below are the first body paragraph and the beginning of the second one; phrasing I refer to later is in italics.

> *Often*, separation *may* not be a new issue between primary caregiver and child by the time the child is old enough to enter school. *Furman (1950) believes* the mother plays a major role in allowing the child to progress developmentally on track, particularly in the early stages. (*In her article, Furman refers solely to the mother's role, believing hers to be the most instrumental among any other possible caregivers.*) One crucial role the mother must take on is the role of *being there to be left*. *For instance,* weaning is a form of separation where the mother is being left by the developing infant. *Furman puts forward the idea* that it is the baby who weans the mother, and not the other way around. The baby provides the cues; the mother must then "heed" the signals of the child and allow the separation to occur. She is *being there to be left*. The baby is then allowed to move on and grow. This task is not easy for mothers; it can be very difficult, especially if she is to endure it repeatedly as the child progresses from stage to stage developmentally. If this is accomplished, positive things *usually* then emerge from the relationship. The baby "soon realizes his new achievement and invites the mother to share in and admire his fun" (Furman 20). The baby must feel free to learn and is reassured that this newfound independence does not harm their relationship. *Mahler (in Crain 2000) further explains* that during the Separation/Individuation Phase the baby is "maturationally driven to develop independent functioning and explore the

wider world" (Crain 302). The mother must endure this sort of rejection; she should view it as "neutralized growth rather than an instinctual battle" (Furman 26). *Furman also asserts that the educators involved in the transition can convey to the mother* that when she is there to be left even at this early stage, she is aiding the "child's mastery of developmental steps and [this] paves the way for neutralized progressive achievement of skills, activities and even functions" (Furman 27).

*Mahler maintains that still another helpful task* for the primary caregiver to perform is to serve as a "home base" for the exploring child. *If we do see the child this way, we can later see the child during what Mahler terms* the Practicing Phase exploring with "bold exhilaration" (Crain 299). *According to Mahler and other theorists . . .*

Allen identified problems with authorship in two genres her students produced: the book report, where writers made little comment on the relationships between ideas, and the response essay, where writers discussed whether they agreed with their sources. Espinoza wrote the research essay because his stance on the material was appropriate for his reader, and we can see this by studying his evaluative metalanguage. Through metalanguage, writers signal to readers their involvement with material (Brandt; Vande Kopple). In my view as a reader familiar with Allen's requirements, Espinoza succeeds because he tells his reader he can use research to frame the problems in children's behavior he encounters in the workplace. Aligning himself (and thus other preschool teachers) with researchers, Espinoza fulfills the social motive of the research genre as Allen defined it for her students in this particular class. But Espinoza's stance also reflects the global requirements of the research essay using APA style; he approximates the social speech educational researchers typically employ.

As is appropriate given Allen's goals, Espinoza does not use specialized lexicon to indicate his involvement with reader or evidence, but, instead, he uses a speech typical of the genre. Through this typical speech, Espinoza shows he views Furman and Mahler as scholars working on shared research questions whose findings build on and connect with one another's. To fulfill his reader's particular expectations in this course, Espinoza aligns himself, the writer, with a research community and its overriding value: developmental (not commonsense) perspectives on children's behavior.

Hedges typically abound in research writing because they indicate that scholars take truth to be contingent and not absolute; this language marks the more rhetorically mature stance of student writers who understand a research community actively makes knowledge (Haas; Penrose and Geisler). In the excerpt, Espinoza uses text connectives like *often* and *usually* and conditionals like *may* to cushion his statements. He says scholars do not state the truth but *assert* or *put forward* particular claims. When he says Furman believes the mother plays a chief role, Espinoza adds, parenthetically, that Furman focuses *solely* on her, an evaluative gloss suggesting he is aware a reader might question this focus on the mother's exclusive status as caregiver.

What one chooses to focus on, as Allen said she explained to her students in class, indicates where one is involved in impersonal writing. In the second paragraph, Espinoza indicates this involvement by linking Mahler and others to Furman's earlier work, drawing a connection that Allen expected to see in these papers ( "According to Mahler and other theorists"). Notably, in the second sentence of this paragraph, Espinoza uses the pronoun "we" ("If we do begin to see the child this way"), which he uses twice more in the following pages I have not quoted. The "we" of Espinoza's paper seems to mean "we, the teachers who read educational research," or perhaps the research community more generally.

Espinoza gestures more explicitly to the teacher's status in the research community when, near the first paragraph's end, he refers to the role early-childhood educators play in easing separation anxiety ("Furman also asserts that the educators involved in the transition can convey to the mother"). In the paper's last sentence, Espinoza highlights this role: "And with the help of other professionals, *like the prepared teacher*, separation may occur successfully, allowing the child to flourish developmentally" (emphasis added). Through his stance, Espinoza tells the professor he has fulfilled the purpose of this genre: for teachers to use developmental research to enrich their work with children.

Espinoza had an advantage over some of his peers in this class because he was a practicing teacher. In Lave and Wenger's terms, though, Espinoza was a newcomer to educational research: he had been out of school for two decades; he had an undergraduate degree in the liberal arts, not education; and English was not his first language. Espinoza's strong identification of his writing role with his identity as a teacher seeking further education may have made the genres in Allen's class more socially meaningful to him than was the case with some of his peers. It also appears Espinoza grasped the social motive of the research genre through the social situation Allen made possible for the students in her class. He told Wilson he drew his topic from class discussions based on students' ongoing research; he stressed, too, the benefits of informal writing early in the semester and of Allen's detailed written feedback on drafts he wrote later on.

Espinoza said he would use what he had learned in Allen's class "over and over again in my teaching career." Certainly, he seemed to find the writer's role for the research paper congenial, and he did not, he said, have trouble interpreting what Allen meant by "critically discuss" research using "your own words." In my view, Espinoza, a newcomer to this situation, succeeded because he had the opportunity to practice rhetorical skills in a lively social group; and Marcos Espinoza left Allen's class perceiving he learned something from research he could apply to his work with children, fulfilling the social action writing performs in Vivian Allen's class.

### STANCE IN THE CONCERT-REVIEW GENRE

As I've suggested, the global motives of genres are linked not just to disciplinary but also to a course's professional and institutional aims. Allen described the social motives of her assignments in the distinct context of a teacher-certification program: all her students were enrolled in her class so they could receive a powerful credential in New York state. By some contrast, in general education, professors encounter what is arguably a less well-defined rhetorical context because they assign genres for students who, required to take the course, usually do not intend to major in their special fields. The extent of the teacher's disciplinary expertise is often conflicted in general-education courses, and this conflict affects which genre teachers assign and the sometimes mixed motives they ascribe to assignments (Russell and Yañez).

For one assessment of general education, we conducted a comparative study of the concert reviews students wrote in two music classes taught by the same professor, Dominic Rizzi. Rizzi requested a fellow so he could develop a new approach to the concert review, a standard genre in music-appreciation classes. He hoped, he wrote on his application, to shift this assignment from an academic to a more journalistic emphasis he felt was appropriate for a music-appreciation course.

In her portfolio, Suzanne Ofisi, the fellow assigned to Rizzi, documented her work with him over two semesters in the same class. In the fall, Ofisi observed the situation by reading the textbook, tutoring a few students, and attending lectures. For the spring semester, Rizzi decided to assign students to write two essay exams and two concert reviews (a community-based and a classical performance), and Ofisi created materials to support the reviews. Since students cannot write a draft before they attend a concert, Ofisi decided to create a music heuristic to accompany Rizzi's revised prompt (see appendix 3). This heuristic aimed to help students consider their rhetorical situation before they attended the concert, for instance by urging them to listen to recordings or read reviews published in the *New York Times*. In class, Ofisi exposed students to some of the genre's expectations, giving them a description of the genre from a writing guide, reviews from the *Times*, and a parody from the *Village Voice*. After students reviewed a community performance, Ofisi copied two student papers to discuss in class—she brought a graded set of reviews to our study group, too. Additionally, Ofisi gave students a workshop on note taking; in class, they listened to music, and using questions like, "What is the period of the music?" listed on the heuristic, they wrote informal paragraphs.

To assess the second review assignment, I asked five music teachers to describe, on a survey, the review's purpose; rate concert reviews using a rubric; and participate in an interview about their evaluation. On the survey, these readers wrote that the concert review's chief purpose is to encourage students to appreciate the uniqueness of live musical performance. Though they hoped their students would incorporate musical analysis into their evaluations, these teachers said, they usually assigned reviews to expose first-year students to live performance. In the interview, they agreed the genre caused trouble for them as evaluators in general-education courses because even though they knew it does not call for in-depth analysis of musical structure or extensive historical context, still they valued this expertise.

These teachers also said they distinguished between the reviews they evaluated largely by the quality of the writer's "voice," the word they used. After they scored the reviews, I asked the teachers if the rubric we used was sufficient, and they said that "voice," not an explicit category on the rubric, was significant for them in judging the quality of papers. They spent some time distinguishing between "voice" and "evaluation of the performance," the phrase from the rubric I developed with the fellows. The teachers thought the two were related but not the same because "evaluation of the performance," in the sense of describing its overall worth for prospective audiences, could, they considered, call for more expertise than most students in a first-year course possess. For this reason, they thought the review, more of a workplace than a disciplinary genre, sometimes elicits mixed responses from readers.

I later refer to the added, italicized phrasing in the teachers' consideration of voice in concert reviews.

JANE HAMILTON: *Describing what they got emotionally from the music* [is important]. So if that is left out, then it becomes very dry, I think, more—

IRENE KATA: And you just feel like, they're, *they're not saying anything.*

MICHAEL PEREZ: *Like they weren't there.*

KATA: Right, *like they weren't there.*

CLARA BOWLING: *And I feel like even if they didn't use as much terminology*, but they really, you know, they *engaged*, and they, you know, described it on some level, and they understood it, to me that's a lot better than, you know, just throwing out the terminology and misusing it. . . . Well, *their voice is coming out*, and if they don't do that then they aren't, *they aren't a part of what they're writing at all.*

For these readers, a reviewer's appropriate degree of involvement with the material is personal ("describing what they got emotionally from the music"). Without this engagement, even the writer's appropriate use of terminology is less meaningful to these readers. This distinction between terminology and engagement makes sense in the context of how these teachers define the review's social action: to capture the fleeting uniqueness of live performance, as the individual listener experiences it during the event.

For this reason, the writer's response to the music is unique, compatible with analysis of music but not reducible to it.

HAMILTON: *Don't you find that voice is also connected to content?.* . . . And the ones who were more, who did evaluate or do some kind of analysis, were much more . . . well they were liable *to give their impressions more* or something.

PEREZ: Yeah, and there was *an engagement of the music rather than a simple engagement of sort of the mise-en-scène of being at Carnegie Hall or whatever.* And it doesn't have to be sophisticated, but there has to be some effort, I think, to engage the music.

BOWLING: And whenever they give *their own opinions*, it becomes more interesting, I think, in terms of reading.

The readers explained that in their own teaching and in the reviews they rated, some students tended to lavish too much attention on the concert's venue, or "mise-en-scene of being at Carnegie Hall"; earlier in the interview, Bowling called it the "describe the color of paint on the walls" problem. By contrast, successful writers did not dwell exclusively on the venue, the historical background, or musical structure: they engaged with the music, gave "their impressions" and "their own opinions" about the performance.

Nevertheless, these teachers were not satisfied to reduce voice to opinion; a writer's voice could not be defined in purely subjective terms:

> KATA: But they have—the thing is, like when you give your opinion, I feel like you have to support it with—
> HENRI BEAUFORT: Yeah, yeah—
> BOWLING: Some, at least basic description of what you're hearing. 'Cause otherwise you just get the "oh, it was very nice. People played together," you know?

The teachers' metagenre provides complex advice: give an opinion, but do not abandon analysis; put yourself into the writing, but do not abandon description of the music. In part, the teachers' struggle to define the appropriate stance reflects their uneasiness with the status of expertise in general-education courses. In fact, writing guides for music classes Ofisi consulted and included in her portfolio reflect this conflict, too, as some guides advise students to write reports linking a performance to disciplinary concepts, while others tell students to focus on their impressions of the concert in reviews. As I've been suggesting, the confusing atmosphere surrounding the writer's stance also reflects the difficulty that lies in defining typical social languages. In university situations, this speech requires writers to write between their own and an expert's language; few professors encourage students to mimic their language, but they also caution against using informal speech.

To further examine typical language, I looked at the evaluative phrasing students used in the reviews the readers judged to be above average or excellent. The readers rated thirty-nine reviews, and although to some extent all of the papers contained historical information about composers and descriptions of the venue, it was, the readers suggested, "the writer's voice coming out," or how they talked to readers about their evidence, that fulfilled their genre expectations. Below are excerpts from five reviews in which the writers discuss part of a performance. Each review was at least four pages long, and each received high marks from two readers. Written comments from the teachers were optional, but each of the papers I've quoted from elicited at least one remark from a reader about the quality of the writer's evaluation of the performance. In italics is the evaluative phrasing the writers used.

### Martina Rodriguez: Tonhalle Orchestra at Carnegtie Hall, May 8, 2004

*The musician who stood out the most* was the pianist Leif Ove Andsnes who the *New York Times* called "*the most interesting* pianist of his generation." He is a *well-known* pianist with many accomplishments and awards and to see him playing was *very amazing.* The pianist moved *gracefully but aggressively at the same time. He seemed aggressive because he knew what to do and didn't seem afraid to play, and he was graceful because his body flowed with his piece.* . . . *The violins also stood out the most* as they were the second leaders of the Orchestra. *Each violinist moved in such a way that it seemed she was dancing to the music*; each played together but sometimes the front two violinists would play solo, *showing a leadership role.* And last, the conductor also *caught my attention* and he led each musician in a way *I would never imagine. I always thought that the conductor was useless but I was wrong* because I could see every musician was looking at him, waiting for his arms to be raised and it *was like every note was played from his hand movements.* Overall, the performers were *confident and showed enjoyment* as they performed, *transmitting excitement to the audience.*

### Justin Schmidt: Bargemusic, Fulton Ferry Landing in Brooklyn, May 13, 2004

Once again, the instrumentalists have captured the mood *wonderfully.* The pianist Dmitri Alexeev *dives right in and showers* both himself and the audience with notes that both *float and fly* from the keyboard, which is but a thing to be manipulated by his touch. The string trio accompanies him flawlessly, but it is Dmitri's *control, vivacity, and command* that guide and lead the quartet through the rising and falling rhythms, that at times reflect a homophonic texture, but more often, reflect a polyphonic quality.

## Olga Stalkoff: Emerson String Quartet at Lincoln Center, April 14, 2004

The tempo picks up later on in the piece but slows back down as the music repeats. It rises and falls, twists and turns giving the audience a notion of where it's going next but at the same time not knowing what will happen. The violin does a *small repetition that only brings the audience for a quick ride as it reverts to the slow, calm sound of the cello. This little change only brings in more anticipation from the listener. Creating somewhat of a mournful quality when it comes back to the sound of the strong cello that was there when the piece began, the change serves as the dominant preparation to lure the audience back.*

## Eva Manning: Orpheus Orchestra at Carnegie Hall, May 11, 2004

The final song was called "Passo Mezzo e Mascherada," which opens with the violins, bass, and cellos. They open the song with *a flighty, fluttering sound that gave the audience a cheery feeling.* The flute was included, then the French horn interrupted, then finally, the whole orchestra played, including the piano. The composition was then repeated first by the wind instruments, and then by the strings. *The vivacious tempo and crescendo created a spirited air in the auditorium,* and then it led to a decrescendo. The horns entered the song once again, and seemed to signal the orchestra to play *vivaciously* again, finishing out the song with an allegro tempo. When Respighi's composition was completed, the *audience applauded loudly as the instrumentalists exited the stage. The performance was wonderful, creating images of dancing, feasting, and cheerfulness.*

## Muneeb Baker: Murray Perahia, Piano, Carnegie Hall, May 3, 2004

As the piece continued, *I imagined I was dancing with my husband at my wedding, and then, as I opened my eyes and looked around I suspected that many people in the audience were fantasizing also because many had their eyes closed (so did the pianist).* The entire piece is full of romantic scenery. If you really listen closely you can create sounds of your own imagination. You can sometimes hear footsteps, wind, and whispering. Everyone can get a different idea of what is going on. . . . The piece moves in and out of *slow dreamy sections* and into *scary, traumatic scenes.*

In my view, students appropriately project "emotional" engagement through the genre's typical lexis and grammar, which includes using judgmental adjectives, adverbs, or present-tense verbs to describe both performers and performance. Sounds are "flighty and fluttering," notes "float" and "fly," pianists move "gracefully but aggressively." A cello has a "slow, calm" sound; the tempo is "vivacious"; "slow dreamy sections" alternate with "scary," "traumatic scenes." Performers are "wonderful," "amazing," or commanding. Often, reviewers make these judgments in the context of the emotional relationship between performers and audience that could only exist in this unique moment: "I suspected that many people in the audience were fantasizing also because many had their eyes closed (so did the pianist)"; "The vivacious tempo and crescendo created a spirited air in the auditorium"; "the change serves as the dominant preparation to lure the audience back"; "transmitting excitement to the audience." The writer signals her intimate presence in the unique moment of the musical event, often by invoking personal imagery: "As the piece continued, I imagined I was dancing with my husband at my wedding."

Through evaluative phrasing, these writers also tell the readers they have learned to value classical performance. In papers I've not quoted, writers earning high scores often referred, in their last paragraphs, to the uniqueness of their concert experience, usually by telling the reader that this was their first classical concert and that its beauty surprised them in some way. Several noted the superiority of the performance to recordings, which, on the prompt, in class, and on the heuristic, their professor had recommended they listen to before attending a concert. Occasionally, students mentioned, in the body of their texts, how a performance changed their perceptions, as the author of the first paper does: "the conductor also caught my attention and he led each musician in a way I would never imagine. I always thought that the conductor was useless but I was wrong."

These writers solve the problem of typicality always posed by writing genres. Each review is uniquely the student's own since each involved the writer's personal judgments made at a particular moment in time: "I suspected that many people in the audience were fantasizing also because many had their eyes closed (so did the pianist)." But the successful writers also used the evaluative language typical of this genre that can be found everyday in the *New York Times* (e.g., "The *Times* called him 'the most interesting pianist of his generation'"). Like the critics, the students used language that is not incomprehensible to outside readers, only occasionally employing specialized lexicon (allegro tempo, polyphonic quality). And also like the experts, the students often invoke dreamy images to describe peaceful moments in a performance.

As important, the students do something else the experts do: they underscore the uniqueness of a performance in more than one way. One student expressed the uniqueness of the setting: the tranquil beauty of the dying sun and lapping waves while she listened to an evening of Bargemusic. Another remarked he was surprised that he, a young Latino male, enjoyed this performance attended by a mainly middle-aged, white audience. Several students noted how the music appeared to affect the audience, describing the amount of applause, or looks of boredom and delight. When the music teachers discussed the purpose of the review, Hamilton commented at one point, "Without performance, we don't have anything else." The writers' focus on the singular experience is important because, in the view of these readers at least, it is a fundamental disciplinary value.

As Allen observed and linguists who study authorial stance reinforce, "what you choose to focus on," the selection of material, can make the difference between writing a book report and a research paper or between writing a concert report and a concert review. Through their attention to uniqueness, the musician who "stood out" or the intimate relationship between violin and cello, the writers turn "dry" reports into readable concert reviews. In this way, then, the students solved the problem of typicality. They bring their individual perception to the review and thus, paradoxically perhaps, fulfill its generic aims.

### STANCE AND MOTIVE FOR UNIVERSITY STUDENTS

Ofisi reported Rizzi thought his students wrote unusually good concert reviews in both classes, but he awarded higher grades to the students in the section where she worked more directly with them on writing the genre. The outside readers confirmed these judgments: in their interview, they praised the high quality of the papers, especially their general "readability." In a short report, two fellows analyzed the readers' scores, and they found a statistically significant difference between the papers from Ofisi's section and a section where she did not participate (Soliday, "Comparative Study"). Similarly, in their study of papers students wrote in criminal-justice classes, Ken Peak and Mark Waldo claim readers gave the highest scores to essays in which students responded to a well-defined rhetorical situation. In theory, we could argue students in these classes wrote better papers because they participated in a situation rather than wrote about it (Feldman). By participating to a certain extent in the situation, they could grasp motive, and by grasping motive in a social context, they could find the appropriate stance.

Perception research suggests that often when students discuss the writer's role in university writing, they do not endow these genres with purpose and tend to see the official purpose as separate from their own motives as writers. This may be particularly common in professional programs like nursing, where students struggle to imagine the roles university writing will play for them on the job (Ariail and Smith; Leki, "Living through College Literacy"). This was the case in Allen's class and in other education classes where fellows worked with prospective teachers. When we discussed the interviews from her class, Allen and I agreed that, unlike Marcos Espinoza, many students felt, as one student put it, "disconnected" from the first research assignment. Repeatedly, scholars find, as Lee Ann Carroll comments, that students "resist the critical stance required in much academic writing" (67). Further, in general-education courses, students may experience the requirement to write to experts as a contradiction that limits what they learn (Russell and Yañez).

Further, the research suggests students tend to separate the expert's fact from their personal opinions. This is true even, we found, for proficient student writers, those who have earned the consistent high regard of their readers across situations. Nicolai Menkell, an accomplished writer and an English major whom we met during his last semester at City College, said he thought his teacher's emphasis on analytical genres prevented him from fully appreciating literature. On a midterm survey, which he completed in a science class for nonmajors taught by one of our partners, Menkell reflected, "For me, writing for this course has been very different from my English courses. Ironically, my English teachers require very strict analysis, while this course encourages me to share my *views and opinions*" (emphasis added). More often than we perhaps realize, students invest themselves in composing genres when they can align their personal with academic interests (Beaufort; Herrington and Curtis) or, as in the Stanford University study of student writing, when they write for their own reasons to audiences of their choice (Fishman, Lunsford, McGregor, and Otuteye).

Allen's students, however, complicate these distinctions among motives, facts, and opinions. The focal students told Wilson they learned more from the second assignment than from the first. Recall that the first assignment asked them to "critically discuss" sources in "their own words," while in the second, they were required to apply developmental theory to their observations of a child in school. They learned the most from this assignment, the focal students explained, because it allowed them to share their "own views." "I put my own two cents in, like experiences I've had teaching," explained one student; another agreed, "This one was actually your own thinking."

Remarkably, though, this assignment did *not* invite students to share their "experiences I've had teaching"; and in the papers Allen and I read together from her graduate and undergraduate classes, no one offered such experiences. In my view, the students thought this genre elicited "your own thinking" because with this assignment but less so for the first one, they understood how their own goals (to become teachers) aligned with the genre's (to inform their teaching). Allen's students suggest, then, that one way to engage students in their learning is to create situations where students can participate in a meaningful social situation, as they did, I believe, when they went to concerts or applied theory to their observations. Like Eliza, the exemplary science student Christina Haas studied for four years, students consistently suggest their most meaningful learning experiences evolve from participatory situations, in Eliza's case, lab research with a mentor. If genres act as socializing forces, it makes sense students are more likely to develop an appropriate stance by approximating the expert's actual roles.

## STANCE IN THE COLLEGE ESSAY

When I asked Allen and the music teachers to define genres, they could, in the context of sustained discussion, point to a specific social action performed by the genres they assign. However, this question is more difficult to answer when teachers assign vaguely defined classroom genres such as the college essay, sometimes used in general-education courses, including freshman English (Johns, "Teaching Classroom and Authentic Genres"; Wardle, "Mutt Genres"). I want to suggest this genre may be difficult for weaker students to produce because the stance associated with it does not give students access to a typical social language and the roles and focus that go along with the speech. The reader of this genre is equally vaguely defined as a person with some expertise on something, though not necessarily the particular topic, situated somewhere in the university. Most students know, however, that their actual reader does not resemble this imaginary reader, often a teacher with definite disciplinary expertise and generic preferences.

To explore the college-essay genre, I draw on a portfolio from a psychology class several fellows assembled over two semesters. This was a class where fellows did not play a coparticipant role with faculty. For this class, a jumbo course serving hundreds of students, the professor invited fellows to create for students workshops held at the Writing Center. To learn more about students' responses to prompts, he also asked us, in the second semester, to use naturalistic methodology to study the situation. In the first semester, fellows attended lectures and interviewed teaching assistants, studied prompts, talked informally to students, and collected graded papers. In the second semester, one fellow, Joanna Parzik, and I met with the professor and his assistants; following this meeting, Parzik interviewed several teachers and the students from one section and wrote a report for the professor describing her findings.

Since the prompts and the teachers' perceptions of the students' writing remained unchanged over both semesters, I use for my analysis the graded papers from the fall semester and the interviews with students from the spring semester. Though this means that we did not interview the student writers, the generic atmosphere surrounding the writing was, across semesters, so similar that I use Parzik's report to contextualize the graded papers I examined from the earlier course.

The primary metagenre for this course was a series of prompts, to which teachers and students frequently referred. Students had to write at least five essays based on different subfields of psychology, such as cognitive, developmental, social, or clinical psychology. For each prompt, students had to write an essay with an introduction, body, and conclusion and discuss a psychological scenario by using a specific number of concepts (usually three to five) from the lectures and textbook. At the same time, most prompts warned students not to copy the textbook: "Use your own words to discuss the concepts." The fourth prompt I focus on, covering clinical and abnormal psychology, describes the scenario students were to discuss:

Judy's case. As the chief metagenre, the prompt offers the conflicting advice that reflects the difficulty we all have defining what comprises typical speech, warning students to cite outside sources but to use their own words. The metagenre was also shaped, however, by this course's daunting institutional situation. General education poses a distinct rhetorical challenge because genres in these classes are not, compared to courses in the major, as closely tied to disciplinary or professional situations. But also, unlike other general-education courses I consider, this one served hundreds of students who attended a lecture and then were instructed more directly by a corps of inexperienced teaching assistants. Rather than give multiple-choice exams, the usual choice in this situation, this dedicated professor took a risk by assigning several short essays over the semester. The prompts provided students with specific situations to consider that reflect disciplinary experience, but to solve the problem posed by the jumbo class, they also ask students to write essays containing three parts and to discuss a fixed number of concepts.

On the one hand, the prompt I consider features a rhetorical situation and invites writers to imagine their role as a therapist. Judy, the prompt says, is the forty-year-old child of an abusive alcoholic father and divorced parents. Three years ago, Judy's husband died in a car accident, and during the last year, she was passed over for a promotion at work. "When you interview Judy," the prompt explains, "you learn" that she is now drinking heavily, abusing sleeping pills, and withdrawing from family, friends, and children. She beats her young son, who has become withdrawn and is having trouble in school. Additionally, Judy has no appetite, and she does not sleep well at night because she has panic attacks; she may lose her job due to absences, even as her bills pile up; and she cannot stop thinking about her husband. After detailing this situation, the prompt closes with these instructions to write a college essay:

> For paper #4, define and apply five (5) of the concepts listed in Section 4 (Abnormal/Clinical Psychology, weeks 11–13 on your syllabus), to describe Judy's case. You may *explain* the causes of her behavior, *diagnose* her, *treat* her, or any combination of

these (e.g., diagnose and treat her). Paper #4 must be written in essay form; include an introduction and a conclusion. THE ENTIRE PAPER MUST BE WRITTEN IN YOUR OWN WORDS.

The teachers' talk about students' responses to the prompts concerned the problems students had understanding the conventional features of the college-essay genre. After they interviewed the head TA, the fellows reported she thought a widespread problem was that students tended to list definitions from the textbook without comment: "they are not written as coherent, integrated essays." Similarly, teaching assistants in both semesters equated the essay genre with its conventions; the listing problem they consistently identified stemmed, as one reported, from students' "lack of knowledge of how to write an essay." In their portfolio, fellows noted that the head TA hoped students could "integrate definitions and concepts into their own texts organically and smoothly. [The professor] would like students to be able to read the whole assignment carefully, understand the task, and then plan a paper (using a process) that they have conceived, not just follow each step one by one."

Similarly, in the section Parzik studied, the teaching assistant identified that the major problem with the assignments lay in students' tendency to list definitions from the textbook. The students whom Parzik interviewed agreed with this assessment, for they were well aware of the generic atmosphere surrounding the prompts. However, in the view of most, the prompt elicited the listing problem. First, they said they could not reconcile how they conceived the essay genre with the requirement to discuss a defined number of concepts. They ascribed the listing problem to the lack of freedom the prompt gave to writers: "For example, we had to define three concepts on the list, and you had to use them in your essay. But in an essay I can't just do concept one, define, example, number two, define, example, and so on. I have to keep only what is useful for my essay [to] keep the essay moving smoothly."

Second, the students addressed the problem of finding an appropriate stance in terms I have heard students use in other courses: were they supposed to give only the facts or forward an opinion of the facts? Students said they were not sure where to find acceptable opinions about the scenarios, a problem with invention that the next chapter considers. They also cited the requirement "to use your own words" as problematic: to what extent could they elaborate on a definition from the textbook? Where, they asked, do we draw the line between facts and our own ideas and experiences? "They want you to write the definition in your own words. When you try to explain a complicated concept in your own words, you have to be very careful, you know, be careful to keep to the [psychological] meaning." As another student bluntly put the case, "I can only write the facts."

For these students (and their teachers), the essay genre is defined less by its situation or content and more by its conventions: it moves freely between paragraphs and is not constrained by the need to cover a prescribed set of concepts. As Parzik learned, too, individual students in this section said they spent time wondering what kind of thesis governs this essay or what goes into a conclusion for this assignment (a summary or new points?). In their focus on conventions and related to their struggle to define a conventional stance, the students (like their teachers) never explored the question: what is the purpose of this essay for readers? This group of students focused on interpreting the prompt; no one described a process of planning an essay before writing the final draft.

These interviews provide a useful context for my reading of graded papers responding to Judy's case that the head TA gave fellows in the fall semester. One teacher failed Lola Berry's paper (thirteen out of thirty points) because it lacked an introduction; she wrote to the fellow, "This essay is not based on psychological principles; [it is] rather the *writer's own opinions*" (emphasis added). Berry's peers struggled to distinguish between fact and opinion, a struggle that, I have been arguing, is common for university students because the problem of the writer's relationship to evidence is a problem of authorship, or stance. In the absence of supports for writing beyond the prompt and teacher commentary, Berry's paper offers indirect evidence of how some writers approached the problem of basing their essays on course principles.

For most students we talked to, *opinion* means "my personal views, experiences, ideas, and thoughts." Berry's paper, however, presents little of her personal views or ideas. Even though the teacher cited this paper as being especially opinionated, the writer's presence is, linguistically, strikingly minimal; in kind if not degree, it is probably typical of freshman writing whose authors seem to vanish from the text without offering substantial evaluation of material (see Strachan; Walvoord and McCarthy). The three opening paragraphs of Berry's untitled, one-and-a-half-page paper are below. In italics are the evaluative phrasings I refer to in the discussion following.

> Judy suffers from depression. *Ever since her father died*, she has become depressed. There have been *a number of events* leading up to Judy's depression. *The events* started when Judy was just a little girl. Her father was an alcoholic and often beat Judy and her brothers in order to release his anger. *Another event that caused* Judy to be depressed, was when Judy thought she was up for promotion at work; when Judy did not receive the promotion, she began to think she was worthless.
>
> Judy became withdrawn from family and friends. By becoming withdrawn from family and friends, Judy *is now setting that example for her children*. There are many ways which Judy can be helped. Each way concentrates on Judy and each way affects the way she treats the people around her.
>
> One way to treat Judy is group-centered therapy. Client-centered therapy is when the therapist helps the client build up his or her self-esteem. This type of therapy also helps the client to remember how much the people around them love them. This type of therapy applies to Judy in a way which helps Judy to regain what she has lost . . . her self-respect. *Judy needs to help her children get over their fathers' death.*

Though the prompt tells the student "when you interview Judy, you learn" the terrible facts of her case, Berry does not explicitly indicate she is the therapist who has fully considered the narrative. In her paper, she cites minimal details from the prompt, and this elicited comments from the teacher, for example that Berry ignores Judy's problems with drinking or sleeping pills; further, the teacher noted Berry assumes Judy's depression began when her father died, but the prompt does not say he died. The teacher also clarified Berry's confusion between client-centered and group therapy, course concepts the teacher thought she failed to understand.

Berry follows these opening paragraphs with three more detailing the therapies she thinks will benefit Judy: another one on client-centered therapy, a second on drugs, and a third on free-association therapy. After describing the treatment plan, Berry briefly concludes her paper: "The most important treatment Judy needs is love and devotion from her family. Judy is looking to gain attention. She needs the love and support of her mother and the comfort of a friend; with this, Judy can learn to love again and be a better mother to her children." Berry's conclusion prompted several annoyed comments from the teaching assistant, including "Really!" and "!!!!" as Berry draws upon her own commonsense explanations for Judy's troubles. Using her own words, Berry says the most important treatment is the love and devotion of her family, not the psychological interventions that form the basis of this assignment. In my view, the teaching assistant is irritated by these commonsense "opinions" because they show that Berry does not hold "psychological principles" in high regard: no student establishes a bond with a teacher by suggesting the field's principal beliefs are irrelevant.

Like Berry, Antonia Salcedo organized her paper by beginning with Judy's background and then offering a diagnosis, treatment plan, and an opinion on Judy's future. Her six-page essay received thirty points and the teacher's comment: "This is excellent. You really understand the material & Judy's condition!" The teacher peppered the paper, especially Salcedo's frequent references to the details she drew from the prompt, with approving checkmarks; she queried Salcedo only about her specific choice of drugs to treat Judy.

Though she uses everyday language for the most part, Salcedo's paper is suffused with evaluative statements. We can see this by studying the quality of the metalanguage she uses. Hunston and Thompson show how evaluative statements, the textual markers of stance, permeate impersonal academic writing at every level from the word to grammar and whole texts. Recall that successful writers in both early childhood development and music made frequent use of evaluative phrasing in their papers. "Evaluation," Hunston and Thompson claim, "which both organizes the discourse and indicates its significance, might be said to tell the reader the 'point' of the discourse" (12). Writers use nonreferential language, William Vande Kopple explains, to build their relationship to "ideational material" and to relate to readers, guide them through their texts, and project their own attitudes and beliefs (91–93; Barton, "Contrastive," "Evidentials, Argumentation"; Brandt; Groom). In university writing, metalanguage enables students to tell their teachers that they are involved: they have learned something from a course.

In her paper, Berry rarely addresses the reader but indicates her involvement with evidence by chastising Judy (she wants to gain attention, she needs to learn to love her children) and thus adopting the voice of the elder in the community (Bartholomae). By contrast, Salcedo subtly uses evaluative metawords to indicate she believes in the value of psychological principles and, through repeated words and transitional phrasing, signals the causal relationships typical of the case-study genre.

The first two paragraphs of Salcedo's untitled paper follow. The words in italics are those that Vande Kopple describes as epistemological markers or typical phrasing that indicates the writer's relationship to the reader and her beliefs about the status of the evidence.

*My newest patient came in today.* Her name is Judy. She has been having a *rough time of it this year.* Judy was raised in a home with alcohol and physical abuse. She *now* has two kids and was *recently* widowed. In *this past year,* she has been turned down for a promotion at work, and a hit and run car accident killed her husband. Judy is *now* the sole provider for her two children, and the financial strain is hard on her. Judy is taking medication to help her sleep and abusing alcohol. *The recent events in this past year* have not only affected Judy but also her kids. Her son has become withdrawn, disobedient, and troublesome. *I believe I can help* Judy get through these *rough times* with some therapy.

*After only a few sessions with Judy, I believe I can accurately* diagnose her with *general depression, anxiety,* and *posttraumatic stress disorder.* Depression is a mood disorder, which can alter a person's way of behaving. She shows all of the classic signs and symptoms of depression. *Just by looking at Judy, I can see* that she is tired, underweight, and unmotivated. *She has told me* of her thoughts of suicide. She feels her children would be better off without her since she is not a fit enough mother to provide for them properly. Judy gets little if any sleep at all. *In the mornings* she is unmotivated to go to work and has missed a lot of days. *Ever since she was passed up for the promotion,* she feels incapable of achieving her career goals. Judy has low self-esteem and feelings of hopelessness. She rarely sees or speaks to her friends and frequently withdraws from social events. Judy's depression was brought on *when she was passed up for the promotion early on this year.*

Notably, the teaching assistant checked many of Salcedo's references to the time that events occurred, probably because Salcedo builds a causal argument, which she indicates through shifts in time, for instance that "Judy's depression was brought on when she was passed up for the promotion early on this year." These references to the timing of events also help Salcedo to signal to the reader where she is in the essay and to build coherence in her paragraphs. For example, she repeats twice, in the beginning and at the paragraph's end, that Judy is "having a rough time" this year.

On the second page, Salcedo elaborates her diagnoses of Judy and succinctly defines terms from the textbook such as posttraumatic stress disorder. On the third page, Salcedo announces, "I would like to treat Judy in several ways," and proceeds to offer a range of treatment options that elicit several checks and a "good" from her reader. She finishes her essay by offering her opinion of Judy's case:

*In conclusion, my opinion* is that Judy's condition has *deteriorated over the past year, but it is not so severe it can't be fixed.* The fact that Judy has come to me and told me that her thoughts of suicide scare me tells me that she wants help. She wants to get better but doesn't know how to do it herself. Judy wants to get better for herself and her children. Maybe seeing how her son is handling the loss of his father will help Judy to realize she can't dwell on, or relive it, because her son will, too. They need to mourn his loss and move on. She will not have to stay on the antidepressants forever. *I think* with a couple years of family and cognitive therapy, Judy and her family will be just fine.

In her opinion, Salcedo blends her own typical words with those from psychology to evaluate Judy's condition. She says Judy's condition is not so bad "it can't be fixed," her own phrasing, yet judges that the family "needs to mourn his loss and move on," gesturing towards the language of a psychological process. Through this blended phrasing, Salcedo signals to the teacher she believes in the power of psychology to alter the individual's life: with a diagnosis and contemporary therapy, Judy can heal and "move on."

In my view, the less-successful writers in the batch the fellows collected wrote free-floating college essays, which the prompt directly solicits, while the more-successful writers produced case-study essays, which the prompt also, though indirectly, requests. Casting the assignment in terms of its therapeutic situation, these successful writers reconciled the contradictory advice the metagenre uses to describe typical speech: use your own words while referencing the textbook. Right away, Salcedo establishes her role as a therapist who, authoritatively, has considered the details of Judy's life narrative and then, based on the time that events occurred, makes the appropriate judgments. Like other writers earning at least twenty-five points, Salcedo used terms from the textbook to interpret the narrative of Judy's life, thus solving the problem her peers identified of how much she could say about definitions. By contrast, Berry did not use the case as her central source for her essay, and when she did refer to the prompt's details, she sometimes did so inaccurately; consequently, she did not have enough material to make a causal argument based on the timing of events in Judy's case.

In part, I chose Berry's paper to discuss here because, with its marked lack of the writer's evaluative presence, it may be typical of a widespread "listing" problem researchers describe in student writing at their institutions (e.g., Strachan). I want to stress that Berry's peers described how they struggled to distinguish the textbook's fact from their own opinion, a problem of finding the appropriate stance. In the teachers' metagenre for this course, the request "to use your own words," like Vivian Allen's, was meant to warn students not to copy sources but to assimilate them with their own accent, as Bakhtin describes the process. The students the fellow interviewed knew they were not supposed to offer just their own opinions, but they were unsure in that case what to do beyond copying the textbook. Because they could not solve the problem of stance, they focused instead on interpreting the conventions of the college essay; the teachers whom the fellows interviewed also cast the students' problems with writing in terms of their knowledge of the college essay's conventions.

The prompt asked students to apply concepts to a scenario in the format of a college essay, but it also implied students should behave as therapists who apply psychological principles to a case. I'm speculating that students who did not adapt the college-essay form to the situation selected the vaguely defined relationship between reader and evidence that shapes this form. Writers who select a particular genre are also selecting a stance that typifies the genre: this was the case, Allen believed, with many of her students in early-childhood-development classes. If the genre is inappropriate, then so are the writer's typical speech and degree of closeness to both readers and evidence. If a student selects the college-essay form, the details of the case are not a central source for writing, the textbook is. Perhaps more rhetorically savvy, Salcedo wrote what I recognize as a case-study essay, and she perceived and made central as a source for writing the details of Judy's case.

Salcedo solved the problem of typicality the metagenre posed by adopting a wilder stance, as it were: by speaking as a seasoned therapist, she thoroughly engaged her teacher and integrated principles into her paragraphs, achieving the coherence all the teachers said they desired. But smooth transitions are conventions driven by motives; conventions do not create motives. Lacking a sense of motive, several students the fellow interviewed were stalled by trying to guess what an appropriate thesis looked like or how to end their essays. Without knowing why people write case-study essays to begin with and how they approach the task, students were, I believe, less likely to untangle Bakhtin's paradox of genres: to see that "your own words" means using a typical, not an imitative, speech.

## STANCE: DOMESTICATED OR WILD

In his call for composition scholars to study literacy as it occurs in microsituations, Paul Prior distinguishes, aptly, between literacy in the wild and its domesticated versions (152–53). By studying how genres behave in the wild, teachers can craft prompts that invoke the situations of their use, which in turn will help writers to gain a sense of typical speech, imagine their roles, and select their angle of vision. Genre research suggests that students will learn more if they have direct access to well-defined social situations typical of an expert's practice. This is probably the best way to teach stance, since achieving the appropriate angle of vision really involves using a social language. In my experience, the academy's metageneric atmosphere for stance is thick with rules warning students not to use the first person or advising them to write to readers who know nothing about the material. This body of advice domesticates the complexity of stance as I've been considering it here. To speak formally, students may need access to typical language, which includes but cannot be reduced to specialized lexis: we used to call this Engfish, and most professors recognize it as mimicry. We can, I believe, give students richer access to typical speech if we can imagine less-domesticated roles for writers, provide frequent opportunity for a novice to approximate the expert's literate habits, and tolerate students' attempts to approximate expert speech.

Naturalistic research consistently suggests students engage more with assignments where they approximate expert roles and grapple with a field's "true questions" (in this regard, see the excellent prompts Gottschalk and Hjortshoj have collected). Marilyn Sternglass found students experienced transitional points in their college careers when they designed and conducted their own research projects. When asked to choose the most meaningful paper from their four years of college, the students in Carroll's study selected hands-on assignments. As Carroll observes, genres like these require writers to apply concepts from a course to something they observe or interact with in the world; they include the concert reviews or the observing-a-child-at-school essays cited in this chapter (and several referred to in the next). Assignments built around burning controversies or focused questions in a field may have the same impact on college writers (Light; Sommers and Saltz; Waldo).

Perhaps, as Anne Herrington speculates, it is easier to "compose oneself in a discipline" when one is asked to behave like an expert from the beginning, doing the things that experts habitually do and trying on their wilder roles ("Composing One's Self"; Herrington and Cadman). In this respect, then, we can see how Antonia Salcedo crafted a wilder role for herself, for by taking the perspective of the wise therapist, she also crafted a rhetorical situation. By contrast, the domesticated form some of her peers produced reflects an equally subdued role for the writer.

A novice needs steady exposure to the language that experts and peers typically use to establish their relationship to evidence and to readers. In this regard, in our WAC program, we saw that prompts can establish situations but that, equally, the body of warnings and advice may need to exceed the limits of an assignment sheet: the assignment cannot just be given in class but would, ideally, be enacted in some way. Moreover, this body of advice should be informed to some extent by a teacher's consideration of how genres actually behave in the wild. Dominic Rizzi's prompt, embedded in the syllabus, was only a few lines long, asking students to write "journalistic reviews" and promising they would rehearse the genre during class. Despite this brevity, students did not report having difficulty understanding the metagenre. This is probably because the metagenre included some exposure, in class, to reviews written by experts and proficient students alike. From this exposure, instead of writing an essay, a student has a better chance to write a review, a situated form that accomplishes a social action for readers in a field. From some exposure to wilder forms, writers are more likely to guess what social actions genres perform for actual readers.

But, the examples discussed so far also show that the problem of finding ideas to write about is intertwined with finding an appropriate perspective. As Hamilton astutely commented, voice is connected to content. In my experience, writers who produce undeveloped texts do not have much to say to begin with, in which case planning and then writing an essay are irrelevant. Though Salcedo's professor hoped students would plan their essays, the assignments in the psychology class lacked any formal structure for helping students to find ideas and organize their essays, a typical situation even in writing-intensive courses. Teaching stance also requires teaching students how to find ideas and generate telling details before the formal writing even begins. To distinguish between a summary of terms and their interpretation, which was the essential move the psychology students were really pinpointing, a writer has to anticipate what readers need or want to know and why. The next chapter explores these relationships between invention and evidence, motive and readers.

# 3

## Content in Genre

FINDING A STANCE is inseparable from having something to talk about in the first place. But even once writers have material, they must figure out what content readers deem important since in the university, experts view some information as taken-for-granted facts and procedures in their fields. Across fields, teachers frequently ask their students to establish main points or an implied focus, but finding these depends on whether writers distinguish between the novel and the common idea, the broad generalization and the telling detail. Or, it may depend on distinguishing between a theory and the data, an interpretation and a specific case. In these instances, writers must turn *content* into *evidence* for the readers, who will decide the difference.

Genres shape readers' decisions about what typically constitutes evidence in recurring situations. For this reason, turning content into evidence is a social matter, since writers figure out, for instance, what counts as a standard procedure or a main point by guessing what readers already know and expect to learn. What readers want to know is the engine driving the social action the genre performs. Therefore, it makes sense that writers need to have frequent contact with readers so they become familiar with a genre's typical motives.

In their theory of situated learning, Jean Lave and Etienne Wenger show why writers need to have meaningful social experiences with genres to fulfill their readers' expectations. This chapter begins by briefly describing their theory in the context of composition studies, which has long advocated a theory of invention as a social act. Examples from an architectural-history class illustrate how one professor and a fellow wove invention strategies directly into an assignment. Genre researchers show how in the workplace, expert writers invent genres in a busy social context: talking about models or prompts and sharing their writing with readers. Similarly, I offer parallel examples from biology, art, and media communications to explore how writers need to grasp the expectations of particular readers in order to shape their content into evidence. In all these cases, teachers attempted to invite students to participate in situations rather than only write about them.

As Lave and Wenger show in their case studies, individuals learn to do something well when the practice is woven into a social context. In this type of research, the role that overt instruction plays is a conflicted one, with researchers arguing over the extent to which any genre can be explicitly learned, as opposed to being acquired as students absorb the social language of a field. I argue, instead, that what matters is less the amount of overt instruction and more how well professors *contextualize* genres in their classes, aligning the genre's motive with course material, which might include explicit discussions of a field's rhetoric. I conclude my study of genre by describing a professor's successful effort at building this context in an anthropology class.

## GENRE ENTAILS SOCIAL PARTICIPATION

Lave and Wenger's important book *Situated Learning* accounts for how "newcomers" to a social group learn to do something well in the eyes of the group's "old-timers" or "adepts" (see also Wenger). Broadly, Lave and Wenger describe apprenticeships during which newcomers stay on the sidelines, getting a sense of what the whole practice is about and then participating only partially. "Partial participation" requires rehearsing the practice in "segments of work that increase in complexity and scope" (80). Gradually, the learner moves to the center of the social group, becoming an "adept" or old-timer by mastering its practice.

In one case Lave and Wenger consider, Carol Cain's ethnography of Alcoholics Anonymous, the newcomer to the group gains expertise in large part by mastering the confessional genre (80–84). Cain says newcomers do this by being immersed in the typical words, rituals, and cultural models for behavior and identity that this social group promotes. From the start, they are exposed to a steady stream of models, listening to, reading, and talking about oral narratives. At the same time, the newcomers interact with old-timers and gain a place in the group. Without explicit instruction, they begin to tell stories in small parts; when these bits are inappropriate, the adepts just do not pay attention. Over time, if they accept the model of identity AA promotes, newcomers move to the center of the group and master the genre, telling, Cain says, "polished, hour-long stories—months and years in the making" (80).

The alcoholic in AA meetings acquires the genre's preferred narrative structure, the stance and ideological content through partial participation and exposure to models that interaction with the group provides. From the viewpoint of genre studies, we could say that the newcomer to this group gains direct access to the whole genre by practicing it in segments in a talkative social group. By being immersed in the social life of the group, the newcomer understands that a genre is aligned with the group's "ways of doing" (Carter). In this way, a newcomer becomes an expert teller of stories in Alcoholics Anonymous.

There are problems with the apprenticeship model built on an idealized theory of situated literacy, particularly, for instance, its potential lack of attention to how the dynamics of power surely exclude newcomers from participating in a situation, and its exclusion of metacognition as a valuable and probably necessary ingredient of learning to do anything well. But, here I want to stress how situated-learning theory powerfully links a genre to the social experience that makes the genre meaningful from the start. It explains why the invention strategies and sequenced or linked assignments WAC specialists bring to the disciplines are so useful for writers addressing new audiences about new subject matter. Further, the theory justifies why students in college need direct and ongoing exposure to talk about prompts, models, and drafts with *particular* audiences: it explains the difference between participating in a situation and writing about it from a distance. Above all, Lave and Wenger's theory underscores that genre is a social practice defined by the interaction between writers and readers. This is why, as one of the students from a psychology class told the fellow, "The assignment sheet alone wasn't enough."

## INVENTION IS A SOCIAL ACT

In composition studies, Karen Burke LeFevre was the first to theorize that rhetorical invention is a social, not a purely individual, act. Studies of workplace writing similarly document how texts come to life through dense social networks (Bazerman, "Systems of Genres"; Berkenkotter and Huckin; Dias and Paré; Dias, Freedman, Medway, and Paré; Odell and Goswami; Spilka; Tardy; Winsor, "Genre," *Writing*). On the job, expert writers who are responding to a prompt understand their task while they gather their facts and brainstorm ideas; they write recursively as they consult models, talk with peers, and circulate drafts. Immersed in a social situation, professionals often generate and shape their material by learning what their readers expect to know.

By contrast, basic writers in college struggle to generate material (Mina Shaughnessy observed that brevity is a hallmark of their texts), and they lack social experience addressing expert readers about new subject matter. Lacking enough to say, many students fall back on their commonsense knowledge. Even an accomplished nursing student struggles to find something to say to specialized audiences to the point, Jennie Ariail and Thomas G. Smith document, that she strings sources together without evaluative comment. Though composition teachers reclaimed invention from ancient rhetoric in the 1960s, this art is still largely neglected in the prompts I have seen teachers prepare across disciplines. In our WAC program, we often worked with faculty who told students, either in class or on an assignment sheet, that they needed to follow a process for collecting information before they composed their texts. But we rarely saw professors structure invention so that this art was central to the assignment or closely linked to what occurred in class.

In the arts, professional schools, laboratories, and behavioral sciences, professors frequently ask their students to apply concepts from lecture to quantitative data, human and animal behaviors, the natural world, and to cultural events, texts, or objects. For instance, genres like the case study, widely assigned in business, the behavioral and social sciences, and some humanities classes such as philosophy, ask students to apply broad concepts to a specific narrative. In this situation, expert writers compose the genre *while* they gather their observational data or during the process of studying the course concepts they apply to the case. But as the fellow discovered when she interviewed students in the psychology class, novice writers do not always begin the genre at this point, and this is one reason why writers struggle to move beyond a brief summary of information or their own opinions.

To address this problem, in a jumbo architectural-history class, the professor and her fellow decided to build invention strategies directly into an assignment as part of the whole grade. The professor asked the students to study the Seagram Building and Frank Lloyd Wright's Little House at the Metropolitan Museum of Art. For the Seagram Building assignment, she and her fellow experimented with a genre that resembled the students' private architectural sketch-books, filled with their ideas and drawings. The Seagram Building prompt "segmented" the parts of the whole assignment:

- Draw the building
- Take notes relating architectural form to materials, physical space, and plan of building
- Define *new objectivism*, and write a paragraph about whether it applies to the building
- Write a "preview" to an architectural magazine outlining your argument for how the Seagram Building illustrates corporate modernism

In several disciplines, the fellows created field-guide and journal assignments that students could use to record their observations, define course concepts, and explore their reactions or responses to events on the spot. There is some experimental evidence that this structured invention, for example in journal assignments, leads to better formal writing (MacDonald and Cooper). In our program, fellows developed extensive field-guide materials for students to use in classes ranging from the biology of education to the philosophy of art. In the latter case, the fellow developed assignments to scaffold a formal essay in which students had to apply aesthetic theory to artworks (see appendix 4). To prepare them for this analysis, the fellow developed a "preliminary art-viewing exercise" followed by an annotation exercise of a difficult text. These invention exercises resemble the Seagram Building assignment in that students took notes about an object and defined concepts in response to structured prompts before they wrote a more formal genre.

Carlos Garcia, a student in the architectural-history class, explained how the invention strategies built into the Seagram Building assignment affected his understanding of content:

> *If you're listening [in lecture], you can easily repeat what someone says, but not if you have to write it,* now you have to stretch it, you have to pay attention, so if they use brick here and dark wood on this place, now you have see, how does it look? Because now they're going to ask you, did the materials really complement? Now you have to look and see. In the classroom, she'll tell you, "It's complementary." But when you have to see it yourself, *now you have got to make a judgment call, so now you have to pay attention in a different sort of way.* (emphasis added)

Garcia suggests that a course concept like "complementary" is somewhat domesticated, not the same as actually studying it in the wild. Because he is required to study how the concept actually behaves at the site, he has to "stretch it, and pay attention," "to look and see" for himself how the building relates to terms like *new objectivist* or *corporate modernism*. Writing while he is gathering evidence at the site spurs him to think in a "different sort of way," making "a judgment call" or inference about evidence (as an architect might do). Finding ideas to write about while gathering information is also a "different" way to "see" the information—to gain a position on it. Moreover, Garcia and his peers in this class indicated they felt more like "real architects" when they were asked to write while they were at the site, again stressing the importance in students' perceptions of being asked to behave like experts and try on their roles.

Case-study research suggests that university students read much more than they are assigned to write (Beaufort; Haas). But when novice writers are confronted with a large, and alien, body of material on new topics, especially library research, they often postpone writing their assignment until they have finished the reading. By contrast, professionals start to formulate what they want to say while they are gathering their material, the fundamental, expert move that, again and again, students across the disciplines neglect (Marsella, Hilgers, and McLaren; Walvoord and McCarthy). Often, then, students end up transporting chunks of material from sources to their papers, creating "the book report" genre Vivian Allen described that lacks an evaluative point of view.

The fellows tried to address this problem by annotating articles and discussing in class how experienced writers begin a genre while they are reading. They developed informal-writing assignments for which students had to annotate research articles before they wrote their research or source-based essays. Especially in upper-level classes, students we surveyed praised these annotation workshops where fellows showed them how to start writing while they were reading. A professor in mathematics education e-mailed me after a fellow gave an annotation workshop to report his students met him after class to wonder why they had not received such guidance earlier in their college careers. In a media-communications class, which I describe below, a student told a fellow, "The annotation [workshop the fellow gave] was very helpful. I've actually started to annotate now . . . most of the notes that I have for the paper on my research, I write notes like 'include this in paper,' 'expand on.' So I find myself doing that now."

One of the music teachers I interviewed, Jane Hamilton, observed, "Voice is connected to content." We met many students (and teachers) who tended to think the angle of vision emerges at a later point in the writing process, but expert writers invent the genre when they are writing themselves notes about which telling detail they want to include and/or expand on in their future papers. If we acknowledge invention as necessary to a practice, many students who give their opinions may find, instead, that they have more to say about course concepts and principles.

## READERS AND KNOWLEDGE

Deciding what to expand on or to exclude depends crucially on distinguishing what readers already know from what they want to learn. In part, learning how much information readers need is learning about audiences and who they are, essentially social knowledge about who qualifies as "a general" as opposed to an "expert" reader (Giltrow, "Genre"). This is why, as I know from my own teaching, students in literature classes often retell a story's plot: they do not know how much context a reader needs. It is also one reason why students sometimes write ungainly introductory paragraphs that postpone the main point.

If novices get better acquainted with an audience, as we saw with the example of Alcoholics Anonymous, they also get acquainted with the situation and thus with the social motive the genre performs. If writers can interpret motive, they can also begin to anticipate what an expert reader considers good information. But, as we might expect, no prompt can exhaustively describe what is common knowledge or what information needs to take priority in a genre. Describing the typical reader for university students is especially vexed. Perhaps this is why, as Janet Giltrow finds in her research (and we, too, heard frequently at City College), so many professors advise their students to pretend to address "know-nothing readers," who are not acquainted with the material ("Meta-Genre"; Wardle, "Mutt Genres"). However, pretending the expert reader is not really an expert can lead the novice to assume that commonplace knowledge is equivalent to specialized knowledge. And, of course, the advice is conflicted, because in reality, the actual reader who evaluates the text is a specialist in the field.

Some novice writers may be better able to approximate what experts know if they have grasped the social action that genres perform. For instance, in lab reports students wrote for biology classes at City College, we saw novice writers had trouble distinguishing whether an item was a standard procedure that did not need to be described or a detail that experts expect to be included. But the students' ability to judge the appropriate level of detail seemed also to be linked to how well they had grasped the genre's rhetorical motives.

Over two semesters, several fellows worked in more than one biology course required for majors and for premedical students. In both semesters, students performed a lab experiment of plant photosynthesis and respiration. The students drafted each part of the lab report and received commentary from their peers and their professors, Ben Burton and Lisa Greenberg. Below is part of the first paragraph from a student's draft of the methods section; the italicized sentences are the ones that Burton, the professor for this lab, reacted to.

> First *the YSI meter* was calibrated *in the following manner*: while the probe was connected to the meter, the selector switch was turned to zero; this was also done on the parts-per-million scale (ppm). Next the selector switch was turned to Full Scale, which was set to 15 ppm. Then the membrane on the probe was moistened, and the selector was set to *Calib 02*, after five minutes the polarization of the membrane was complete, and the scale was adjusted to be slightly above sea level. *After this was completed the YSI meter was considered calibrated.*
>
> *A glass jar was taken* and placed right side up into a glass culture dish. The culture dish was filled quarter way with water. Then an elodea plant was placed inside the jar, and a cylinder was placed above it. A magnetic stirring rod was placed on top of the cylinder and water was added slowly into the jar as to prevent any bubbles from remaining. After the jar was filled almost completely with water the YSI probe was tightly screwed to the top of the jar, making sure that *the probe is immersed* in the water.

Burton's written comments concerned which details were missing and which were unnecessary. There were *two* YSI meters, not one, he wrote, and in the left-hand margin, he added, "You could state at first: two identical as described below were set up." Instead of "in the following manner," the expert reader preferred for the student to say, "using room air as the standard." In the right-hand margin, Burton responded to the last sentence in the first paragraph: "This detail is not necessary—calibrating is a standard procedure—refer to instructions or the place where the calibration was 1st described." Similarly, in the second paragraph, Burton changed "A glass jar was taken" to "Glass jars were taken" and "probe is immersed" to "was immersed." On this and other lab reports, Burton frequently distinguished between standard procedures that did not need to be mentioned and important details (two meters; using room air as the standard; glass jars, not a glass jar) that students did need to include.

One fellow, Hugh Givens, worked in biology labs with fellows from several disciplines (English, psychology, and political science) to develop a peer-review process, along with annotation and related informal-writing assignments. An experienced teacher of biology labs at City College (and Burton was on his dissertation committee), Givens had special experience with and interest in teaching the lab report. For this reason, he spent hours in the lab observing the peer-review process, studying drafts, and contemplating what happened in reports he sent to me, Burton, and the fellows. He included these reports and a transcript of a class discussion in his portfolio.

In these reports, Givens concluded that students had trouble managing the "proper level of detail," and he suggested this was connected to their understanding of the social actions genres perform:

> There were two aspects of the Methods section which many of the writers and [peer] reviewers had problems [with]. First was the problem of the proper level of detail. Some included too much detail. For example, several writers went into procedure-level descriptions of how to use the computer program: click this, click that. A few sentences telling the reader what the program does and how the computer was connected to the experimental jar may suffice. *The difference between a Methods section and a protocol should be emphasized.*

Givens emphasized the difference between a methods section and a protocol because, in more than one lab, the professor and other fellows similarly noticed students often confused the protocol with the methods section. Students who wrote a protocol tended to reproduce the format and tone of a cookbook recipe. These students listed the materials on the top of the page, as one finds in a cookbook, and then wrote commands, often using the present tense and conditional verbs that Burton marked as inappropriate. The segments of one student's text where he focused his comments are in italics:

> *The purpose of this part of the lab is to describe the protocol of the experiment and list the materials used.* Calibrate the YSI oxygen meter (model 51b) according to the calibration instructions attached to the lab. To read o2 concentration, set the switch to Temp and read the meter on the appropriate scale. Set the o2 Solubility Factor dial to [the] observed temperature *for fresh water.* Read o2 in ppm. Then remove the cylinders from the jars and place elodea plants in the jars covering them with the cylinders and filling the apparatuses with water (keeping out air bubbles). Next place the magnetic stirring rods on the grids of the cylinders. Place the jars on the stirring plates in culture dishes filled with water about one-fourth of the way up from the bottom. Set the stirring plates on a moderate stirring speed and then cover the tops of the jars with the oxygen sensors and cover one of the jars with tinfoil. Then finally place both jars an equal distance from the *UV* light source. Record the o2 ppm and the temperature every 15 minutes for about 75 minutes. The water in each jar is to be measured separately in a graduated cylinder and results should be recorded. Then the elodea plant *should* be dried and weighed and the results *should* be recorded. *This concludes the experiment.*

Burton drew lines through "for fresh water," "UV," and "This concludes the experiment," unnecessary details for the expert reader, though he wondered, "Why didn't you add the calculation description?" which did need to be included. Burton also drew question marks after *should* and explained, at the bottom of the page, why the verbs were inappropriate: "The writing is choppy and not much of a narrative. The voice changes. Everything should be past tense."

In part, the students' problem with grasping the motive of the methods sections was intensified by the metagenre, in this case, the specific wording on the peer-review sheet the fellows had prepared. For the methods section, one of the questions asked peer readers to evaluate whether the writer had "listed" materials and equipment. In another lab, a fellow wrote in her report that a student asked Burton if they were supposed to list materials in the methods section. In response, Burton explained the section should be written in a narrative mode, and over the next year, he and one of his colleagues revised the peer-review sheet in light of this and other problems students had with the wording. Notably, he and Greenberg also gave students an exercise for writing the methods section (see appendix 5).

In the meantime, the students who chose the wrong genre confused generic motives, since a protocol aims to show a reader how to make something but a methods section narrates what happened so the reader can verify the test of the hypothesis in the lab. Consequently, some of the biology students did not *narrate* the events that occurred but, as the student commented, "*described the* protocol of the experiment and *listed* the materials used." As with Vivian Allen's students who wrote reports instead of research essays, students who selected the wrong genre also selected an inappropriate angle of vision on their material.

As Givens remarked, students who chose the protocol above the methods genre also had trouble figuring out the appropriate level of detail. Givens elaborates on the problem Burton noted in his comment to the student who explained a standard procedure for calibrating the YSI meter, which his audience for the lab-report genre assumes is common knowledge. Not only do students have to find ideas to write about but they also have to figure out which details are appropriate to the genre. In other words, they have to learn to treat content as evidence for expert and not know-nothing readers.

Instead of describing standardized procedures, the students had to supply the rationale for certain steps for the photosynthesis experiment whose hypothesis they were testing. These steps, Givens observed, were missing in many of the reports and constituted the second major problem with the content: "[T]he need for rationales for steps that are not necessarily obvious. Why weigh [the] plant? Why measure [the] volume of water? Why stir water? Why cover [the] plant with tinfoil? Why use ice? Why shake electrode vigorously?" How to include information that is "not obvious" cannot be described on a prompt or in a writing guide (the students had one for this class) because to anticipate everything a reader knows is impossible. Guessing what readers already know is social knowledge gained through interaction in the lab with peers and teachers.

Givens thought the answer to the problem of appropriate detail lies in understanding what audiences need to know. He suspected that motive related to audience in this case because, as he wrote in his report, he had told students in this particular lab to think of their peers as the primary readers for the lab report. Now, he understood it was a mistake to identify peers as a substitute for the know-nothing audience. He had suggested this audience to the students because he reasoned that if students thought they were writing to each other, then they would include more details he did not need himself as a reader. "Perhaps it'd be better to have them think their audience as undergraduates at another university," he speculated, "who may, or may not, have the same equipment. *Just give the reader enough detail to reproduce a test of the hypothesis*" (emphasis added).

Tellingly, Givens links the level of detail to the genre's motive: readers need enough detail to reproduce a test of the hypothesis. But, it matters who the reader is imagined to be. Further, Givens acknowledges that the motives of the expert are mixed with those of the teacher: "I emphasized [the importance of supplying the rationale for procedures] when teaching [Biology 109] not only because good Methods explain why they are, but also because it made sure students understood the reasoning behind the steps in the procedure." In this genre, the writer has to give enough detail to reproduce a test of the hypothesis, but there is also an institutional purpose—the teacher wants to know if the students understand the reasoning behind the procedures.

In school, students are expected to display knowledge for teachers, and this expectation can create conflicts in how experts assess student work: an expert does not need to hear about standard procedures, but, nevertheless, she wants to know the novice has grasped their importance. In our WAC program, I often saw this conflict at work when professors evaluated student writing, and it complicated their efforts to "simulate" workplace genres (Freedman and Adam), for instance, concert-review essays from music classes. As the music teachers told me, they had mixed feelings about writing to general audiences because this meant students did not have to display as much textbook knowledge. In the biology lab, the confusion students experienced when Givens defined a new readership for them only underscores the subtle and complex social relationships to readers that affect how writers turn content into evidence.

## TALKING ABOUT MOTIVE

When reading student work with faculty, I have noticed that although teachers have an idea of what constitutes an exemplary genre before they evaluate writing, they also develop their expectations further when they start to read a set of papers (see also Prior). This is yet another reason why to understand what counts as evidence writers need to make consistent contact with *particular* readers and to judge from this interaction how rhetorical purpose shapes information into appropriate evidence. In Cain's study, the newcomers to AA grasped the structure of oral narrative largely through acquiring the purpose for telling confessional stories. They gained this sense of purpose by discussing models with experienced storytellers in a lively social group. Similarly, the workplace research referenced above shows how experts acquire purpose by writing in dynamic groups where (in these studies, at least) they have immediate access to readers. To find their ideas to write about and to learn what readers expect, experts interpret a prompt recursively while they talk continuously to others, annotate what they read, consult models, and respond to feedback.

Conversely, in the university, genres are often isolated from the social worlds that produce and sustain them. Across fields, teachers tend to view the learning of genre as a linear, static, and somewhat lonely process: students read a prompt, find their evidence, and write a text. Especially in large lecture courses, students rarely get the chance to use the language of a field and to speak about course concepts, even though so many professors say they value their students' ideas and do not want information repeated back to them.

When asked to recall what courses they learned the most from, seniors in the Harvard Assessment Study pointed to small classes where they debated ideas, wrote continuously, met in study groups, and received feedback from teachers or peers (Light). Similarly, when we asked City College students what were the best supports they received for writing their assignments, they frequently stressed the significance of making contact with readers. Like students in other studies, they pointed to their professors first (Beason and Darrow; Hilgers, Bayer, Stitt-Bergh, and Taniguchi), but the City College students also mentioned the important role of talking to their peers, Writing Center tutors, and family members.

In Andy Wheelock's media-communications class, a course required for the major, students had frequent opportunities to make contact with the professor, fellow, peers, and tutors. In class, students reviewed drafts and wrote and talked about one of the central course concepts, media bias. These students were assigned to meet with a Writing Center tutor whom Wheelock knew, and several also met with Wheelock after class to discuss his comments on drafts and finished work. Peter Ho spoke for many of his peers in answer to fellow Brigid Kelly's question, "What were the best supports for assignments in this class?"

> The best supports were group activities, and going to the Writing Center, just getting feedback from other people. It didn't matter if it was fellow classmates or help from the Writing Center, just getting feedback, getting opinions from other people, "[M]aybe you should change this, or write this differently." And again, . . . it's easier to do it like that than somebody just give you the assignment and you have to knock it out yourself. . . . [A]t the end of the day, . . . you get better help from others than from one-on-one [with] a piece of paper.

Often on tape or film, the students the fellows interviewed recalled conversations about writing they had had with peers, tutors, or teachers in the way Ho does ("Maybe you should change this, or write this differently"). Ho's quotation underscores that genres, which, after all, constitute the responses more than one person typically makes to recurring situations, have a social life. Like the experts portrayed in genre research or the newcomers to AA, Ho did not depend on the assignment sheet alone, knocking it out himself. When Ho thought about the assignments in Wheelock's class, he imagined his readers' typical responses.

When the fellows interviewed Ho's peers, several recalled a day when Wheelock read the introductions from rough drafts of research papers out loud, giving his feedback on the quality of their main points. Yesenia Argentio described the exercise at length, quoting some of Wheelock's typical responses to individual papers. From this exercise, Argentio said she understood for the first time that introductions perform social actions: she realized that the purpose of an introduction in a research essay is "to draw readers in" and that hers did not accomplish this. She said she went back to the Writing Center to try out a new opening and had just begun revising her introduction for the third time when she participated in the interview. Argentio's and her peers' perceptions highlight the intensely social nature of conventional structures, which makes sense since our goal is to ask writers to share ideas with others in language. Because a genre performs social actions, we can see why it is so crucial to illustrate conventions like the main point through social interaction rather than simply telling a writer to "write an introduction that draws a reader into your paper."

Though professors from many fields request students to present main points up front, they tend not to discuss these except to mention their importance, usually on an assignment sheet or syllabus. But to confine this convention to a metagenre is not always enough to elicit the much-desired main point. To bring this convention off the page in Howard Shortz's introductory art class, the fellows asked students to discuss the quality of three different introductions written by their peers for an upcoming assignment (the exercise is in appendix 6). For this assignment, students had to compare and contrast two paintings at the Metropolitan Museum of Art. During class, the fellows gave small groups of students three sample introductions from their peers' rough drafts to read and discuss. The first introduction described two paintings of the Virgin and Child in some detail, the second narrated the writer's experience going to the Met, and a third presented a thesis statement comparing and contrasting the two paintings.

The fellows asked the students to compare the introductions by considering the tone of each one and to decide which they thought drew readers in to read the rest of the paper. Here is an excerpt from one group's discussion at the beginning of the exercise, which the fellows taped, transcribed, and included, along with the exercise, in our faculty handbook. The students are discussing the first introduction, where the writer describes each painting in detail:

MARIA KING: The intro's too, um, detailed. There's nothing that drags it along. There's no good tone, you know.

OBI ONO (interrupting King): Another thing it doesn't express any kind of feeling of what the person thought (pause) about the painting.

KING: That's a very good point.

ONO: It just states facts.

CARMEN RIVERA : Well, did you write—are you supposed to write an opinion?

KING: Well, I mean, you know, if—

AEYSHA HUMPHREY (interrupting King): Yah, isn't that the— what the art paper is supposed to do?

KING: It could have. Well, one of the questions on this paper—

ONO: Like when you say art, you're supposed to feel something; you're supposed to get some kind of feeling out of it. (Henriksen et al. 34)

In the group, the students explore Humphrey's central question: what is the art paper supposed to do? As they discuss the genre's motive, they consider one of the chief problems with writing genres identified in chapter 2, how to distinguish the facts from the writer's opinion. From this discussion, these students decide that the first introduction was improperly descriptive, lacking "any kind of feeling of what the person thought about the painting."

As they continue to consider the papers, the students give names to each one of the introductions: the paper with the "feelings" and "thought" they dub the "vision" paper, whereas the descriptive paper they nominate "the details or facts paper." The narrative opening where the writer tells how she got to the museum, they call the "giving directions" paper.

> KING: So this one, it's the *facts,* right? And then the other one, it's the vision. So if we could melt these three papers together, we'd get a good paper, is that what you're [Ono] saying?
>
> ONO: No, not with this [third paper].
>
> KING: Not with this? Why shouldn't you put directions to the museum?
>
> ONO: No.
>
> KING: What if you wanted to go to the museum?
>
> ONO: Put like a, map behind the paper.
>
> KING: You know what I think? *I think this person really did not know what to write about and they started using big words to sound smart,* you know? I know I do that on other papers a lot. (Henriksen et al. 35)

After King makes this observation, she, Ono, Humphrey, and Rivera go on to make a judgment about the rhetorical worth of the three paragraphs. They decide that the first one, the detailed paragraph, and the second one, a story about the writer's experience, are not equivalent to the third, which presents "a thesis." Ono concludes:

> I like this one better than the other one. Because it was like [King] said—it was like an introduction to what the entire paper is gonna be about. He set it up so that he can do one painting, talk about that, go onto the next one, compare them and contrast them, and then his conclusion would sum this up.

As King observed, students might fail to present the main point because they do not have enough to say about a painting in the first place. Recall that the music teachers whom I interviewed identified a similar problem in concert reviews: the tendency to focus on the venue for a concert rather than on the performance. In both cases, the faulty thesis may result simply because a writer does not have much to say about the cultural event, text, or object in question.

Once writers have begun to compose the genre by gathering details or brainstorming ideas, they have to figure out what to include and what to leave out. The accomplished English major whose case Faye Halpern describes from the Harvard Assessment Study had difficulty, for instance, distinguishing details from true disciplinary questions. To find a true question, writers may have to understand, as these students in the art class say, "what the paper is supposed to do." If, like Wheelock's student Yesenia Argentio, they understand what the convention is supposed to do, they can more appropriately consider the relationship between the facts and their feelings or ideas about the topic. One way to get acquainted with the genre is for writers to consider their reactions as readers to a model text: aren't you supposed to get the writer's feeling about the paintings from the opening paragraph? It is surely true that we should be cognizant of the developmental constraints on whether novice writers produce analytical statements. Still, if we lament our students do not approximate them often enough, this may be because, as I have tried to show in this example, we do not ground genres in the social contexts that give them a meaningful purpose.

## ALIGNING COURSE CONTENT AND MOTIVE WITH GENRE

Lave and Wenger argue that in apprenticeship situations, newcomers learn a practice without direct instruction from old-timers. In WAC circles, a related claim that students learn genres by absorbing the languages of special fields has sparked heated debate (Fahnestock; Freedman, "Show and Tell," "What"; Waldo; Williams and Colomb). This debate is relevant beyond these narrow circles, though, because it raises the question of whether anyone can teach writing at all. From my perspective, in AA as Cain describes it, one reason the newcomers learned the confessional genre without direct instruction was because the social group had tightly aligned the genre with content and rhetorical purpose. Similarly, in successful partnerships at City College, we saw that the professors wove their assignments into the whole course: prompts were closely aligned with the course goals and its content, with criteria for grading and the teacher's feedback, or with the daily life of the class. In AA or a college class, the novice acquires genres as a practice when goals are aligned with stance, structure, and content. Novice writers are more likely to be successful when teachers invite them to participate directly in a social situation that gives life to the genre in the first place.

Rather than debate whether teachers in the disciplines should provide more or less "explicit instruction," we could explore whether they adequately *contextualize* a genre in their classes (see also Carter, Ferzli, and Wiebe). In my view, the richest contextualization involves how well professors align a writing assignment with other aspects of the course, and this would not exclude asking writers to reflect on what they are learning or to explore the rhetoric of a field. Recall Rebecca Hatfield, who believed she and her fellow had achieved this alignment when they integrated writing instruction into the content of her advanced psychology course. To do that, she said, she aligned her course goals in an experimental-psychology class with her assignments. Notably, this alignment did not exclude overt instruction, as the fellow prepared a detailed handout describing for students the different conventions in a standard literature review in the scientific article. In class, students applied this handout to evaluate a literature review written by a proficient student, so that the genre was contextualized in a situation of its use. The fellows created a similar modeling exercise for biology, where students are asked to apply conventional features of scientific writing to assess the strength of various examples (see appendix 5).

Brigid Kelly, an accomplished fellow from CUNY's urban-education program who worked with Wheelock's media course, argued in a report that students thought they learned the most when fellows linked rhetoric to the goals and material of a course. Analyzing interviews from three courses, Kelly observed that the CCNY students said they did not learn much when fellows conducted exercises that seemed focused on teaching the writing skills without reference to content or to the major assignments. For instance, in the architectural-history class cited earlier, all the students fellows interviewed said a paragraph exercise the fellow had conducted was unhelpful because they could not see how it would improve their performance on major assignments.

Yet, students like Carlos Garcia also thought they learned a great deal from the Seagram Building assignment because they applied major course concepts directly to a situation, in this case approximating the role of an architect who examines a building site. Equally, a student like Argentio formulated an appropriate thesis statement after Wheelock read several introductions aloud to students, commenting on their rhetorical impact. Several of Argentio's peers whom Kelly interviewed also referred to this day as providing what they perceived to be helpful overt rhetorical instruction. In this case, the students could link the general rhetorical principle solidly to the specific situation, the genre of the research essay they were drafting at the time.

In our most successful partnerships, we observed that professors' metagenres included more than a single prompt: they connected their body of warnings and advice to their overall goals. In other words, these partners linked a genre to its social actions in a course or discipline. In so doing, the most successful may also have given their students the opportunity to think explicitly about the rhetoric of their fields. I want to end my study of genre, then, by describing an entire partnership where the professor and fellow linked general principles to a specific rhetorical situation. Their partnership illustrates this important alignment among course goals, material, and a rhetorical view of genre that was characteristic of most courses where fellows played coparticipant roles.

Cassandra Parker, a distinguished archaeologist, and Julia Mitchell, a fellow trained in cultural anthropology, worked together in two sections of an anthropology course that fulfills a general-education requirement at City College. At the semester's end, Mitchell documented their partnership in her portfolio, and all the materials from it that I discuss here are in appendix 1. Traditionally, along with essay exams, Parker assigned two genres in her introductory anthropology courses: the field report and the ethnology. She and Mitchell revised these assignments, and they began by clarifying the prompt's wording. For each genre, they described the assignment's objectives, the process of writing it, and general grading criteria. On the first of three pages, they introduced both major assignments under the subhead "general objectives":

> One of the most valuable insights anthropology affords is the ability to see the "ordinary" in completely new ways. Each of the assignments described on the following pages allows you to do this but through different techniques. The Congo Project allows you to compare human behavior to that of another species altogether, while the *Nisa* Project asks you to compare your own modern-day culture to that of another contemporary society with quite different cultural practices. In each case, you are likely to observe both commonalities and differences between the "other" you are observing and the culture with which you are most familiar—your own. As a result of this comparison, you will be able to see what is most familiar to you with a fresh perspective, whether you are riding the subway, interacting with your family and friends, walking through the park, or taking a course at City College.

Parker presented the assignments as social actions: writing in the field of anthropology aims to change how students perceive cultures in their daily lives. As noted, professors in general-education classes also have rhetorical motives that are not solely concerned with writing in the discipline but with what Christopher Thaiss calls writing in the course, or WIC ("Theory"). For instance, Parker remarked, when I spoke to her about these assignments, that she also assigned the ethnology because in general-education classes, she liked to learn about her students' cultural backgrounds.

For the first assignment, the Congo Project, the prompt explained that the "point" was "to make inferences about gorilla behavior based upon your observations of one of the groups of gorillas . . . and to compare your findings to what you observe in human behavior." Reflecting on what anthropologists do in the field, Mitchell developed invention strategies that helped students to find plenty to write about while they were at the Bronx Zoo observing gorillas and humans. Her note-taking sheets were structured around major anthropological categories of perception (observational setting, positions, and behavior). Students used these sheets while they were at the zoo so they would have plenty of details to draw from later in the writing process.

But gaining plenty of details is not enough, since writers then have to figure out which information is important and how they should organize it for their readers. After students went to the zoo and took their notes, Mitchell developed a mapping-a-field exercise. In class, Parker gave Mitchell time to discuss with the students two models of comparative organization in the context of their field notes. After they discussed organizing notes into a field report, they wrote their drafts, and Mitchell conducted a peer-review session during which students worked in pairs during class.

At midterms, Parker and Mitchell asked the students to evaluate how well these arts of invention had helped them to compose the field report. In both classes, students were overwhelmingly positive about Mitchell's materials, especially the note-taking and mapping exercises. These exercises, they wrote, helped them to focus their observations at the zoo ("I knew what I should pay attention to when I observed"), generate material ("It helped me to think about questions to ask myself"), and structure their drafts ("It helped me to organize"; "I learned how to outline a compare/contrast field report"). A group of outside readers who evaluated their papers agreed with the students on these points: they rated organization and development more highly than any other textual feature (Soliday, "Reading").

But, Mitchell reported, she and Parker suspected the students were too positive about the writing exercises, so, in class, they elicited more critical commentary. From this session, they changed their approach to the second assignment, "an ethnology comparing aspects of !Kung life, as described in Shostak's *Nisa*, with those of your own culture—however you define it." In her process notes, Mitchell commented:

> [Parker] and I have been attempting to integrate some of the suggestions we received in the students' evaluations into our strategies for the second half of this course: less paperwork, more [small and large] group discussions, and more loosely structured writing. Toward that end, we conducted an in-class exercise on the concept of "culture" in both sections last week, which frankly went fantastically.

Because this exercise was so successful, Mitchell wrote it up for the other fellows as an example of an informal-writing assignment linked to the high-stakes writing expected later in the course. In "Thinking about Culture" (see appendix 1), Mitchell contextualized an abstract definition of culture, giving students the opportunity to talk and write about a major course concept in advance of producing the ethnology. Along with a note-taking exercise, for which students generated details from Shostak's book and their own experiences, "Thinking about Culture" helped students to apply the concept of *culture* to their own lives. This, of course, was a major course goal, as described on the prompt.

Since some students thought working with a partner during peer review had not been helpful, for the next review, Parker and Mitchell decided to take a student's draft from the class for discussion. Mitchell described this exercise for future fellows, too, and reported in her portfolio on what happened when she displayed the student's rough draft on the overhead projector:

> The students actively and enthusiastically participated in the discussion, and we were able to come up with a "map" on the chalkboard of key aspects of the sample text that made it a readable, interesting paper. The students were also able to successfully abstract from this particular piece to ethnographic writing in general, which led to a discussion of the postmodern turn in anthropology, including issues of anthropological authority and cultural conflict discussed in a previous exercise

["Thinking about Culture"]. In the afternoon section, students were far less willing to participate (as they typically had been all semester) and required far more structured (even leading) questions about the text. Ironically, the afternoon exercise eventually led to a discussion of the gaps, problems, and silences in the ethnography *Nisa*, which students were assigned to compare with their own cultural backgrounds.

In both sections, the students talked about content in the context of anthropological stance. The model draft sparked discussions about anthropological authority and cultural conflict, which, in Mitchell's view, the textbook simplified. Though the students in the second section had, Mitchell thought, to be prodded into discussion, nevertheless their talk took an ironic turn because they ended up critiquing the writer's role in Shostak's text. Again, this pleased Mitchell because she had identified similar problems in this ethnography herself.

On this day, Parker and Mitchell selected for discussion a draft written by Johti Vilnu, who compared Shostak's book with her experiences growing up in India. She organized her untitled, six-page draft around three of the seven categories of anthropological perception Mitchell listed on the note-taking sheet: marriage, raising children, and gender. Here is Vilnu's introduction, followed by part of the first body paragraph:

> The !Kung are a group of people that live near the Kalahari Desert in Northern Africa. The !Kung's way of life is captured through *Nisa: The Life and Words of a !Kung Woman* (2000). The !Kung culture is very unique in its own way but not that different from other cultures around the world. [Here, Vilnu makes a note to herself: "ADD MORE."] I am from India, and while I was reading the book, I saw many interesting things about the !Kung which were very similar to my culture. For example, their marriage customs, the way they view children, and the role gender plays in their society can be compared to my very own culture, though there are some distinct differences.

In my culture a very long time ago, girls were allowed to be married as young as ten. Sometimes, two children were said to "be for each other," as soon as they were born. Both families would agree that their children would marry when they got older. So in a way, the infants were already engaged as soon as they took their first breath of life. When the children got older, they had to live with it and were not allowed to even show their dissent if they didn't like the other person. My grandmother got married when she was thirteen. One day she went to go take a bath in the lake, and several women dragged her, dressed her, and took her to the temple to be married. My grandmother had no clues to what was going on, and there she was standing next to a man twice her age. My grandfather was twenty-seven at the time. Soon after, she supposedly learned to love her husband, and they lived a prosperous and happy life.

When I interviewed Mitchell as part of the assessment, I asked her why she and Parker chose Vilnu's draft. Mitchell recalled this draft was "readable" because of the stance Vilnu took on her content, displayed most sharply in the opening: "[Vilnu] starts out with this sort of *evidence* and she's pretty critical of that particular part of India where she grew up. . . . [T]here was some illustration, there was *evidence* there" (emphasis added). Months after the class discussion, Mitchell remembered Vilnu's paper because of the dramatic opening example of her aunt's arranged marriage. This is the power of invention, or discovering useful details to focus ideas and persuade the reader that the writer can offer more than information: the writer is presenting evidence, the word Mitchell used twice to describe her memory of the draft.

Further, as Mitchell indicates, Vilnu uses this detail to establish a "critical" stance towards her material, offering a judgment about how traditional marriage practices in India can oppress women. Through the telling detail, Vilnu extends the implied point about the how women's subordinate status in the culture has evolved over time. For instance, on the third page, after detailing the more "liberal and unrestrained" life of the women Shostak describes, Vilnu continues to detail her thoughts about women's changing status in India:

In India, men and women have very different roles in the household and within society. Though things have gotten better for women over the years, there are still certain duties that are instilled in them. For example, the woman is the sole caregiver of the children in the house. Though nowadays she is allowed to have a job, she still has to make sure that her children are in good hands. Long ago, the women were not allowed to have a job. The men were supposed to provide for their family while the women stayed home, cooked, cleaned, and took care of the children. Now in India, working women are more acceptable in society though some men still don't like women working. Women and men also have certain ways they are supposed to act. Women have to be more reserved and respectful to others around them, especially elders. If a woman acts a little outgoing, she may be considered a shame to her family. The blame will be placed on the mother since it is the mother that the children spend the most time with. On the other hand, if a male behaves in a strange manner, the mother is not to blame because a man is supposed to have his own mind and he makes his own mistakes. These mistakes however are deemed as acceptable because they are seen as a part of growing up. Females are not allowed to make many mistakes because they are not supposed to be in a position to make any. They don't really have a life outside of their home. If they choose to go to a school, they can, but they have to come home right after. If a family decides that it is time for the female to get married, she might often have to drop out of school. Males can do basically whatever they want, and both parents support him since he is a man and is able to take care of himself.

Vilnu uses details to fulfill the ethnology's essential rhetorical motive: to see her culture critically through comparison to, the prompt says, "another contemporary society with quite different cultural practices." In her description, Vilnu tells her readers that she has fulfilled the genre's expectations as those are defined on the prompt: "you will be able to see what is most familiar to you with a fresh perspective." The motive drives the presentation of content, which is perhaps why Mitchell stressed twice that Vilnu turns her memories into "evidence."

Not every student wrote a draft (or even a final paper) as readable as Vilnu's. Chiefly, in the view of the outside readers who scored these papers, this was because the average and less-than-average writers found it more difficult than Vilnu did to be critical about their own cultures and tended, instead, to see both cultures in relative terms (Soliday, "Reading"). That said, the outside readers judged the papers from Parker's class to be well organized and well developed, two rhetorical features Mitchell explicitly addressed. Enrolled in a required course, these students—mostly freshmen, some basic writers, and many new immigrants and first-generation college students with complex linguistic backgrounds—had plenty to say to their readers about a field most were probably encountering for the first time, writing regularly during class and writing two lengthy papers outside it (ranging from five to fifteen pages for each assignment). As important, on the final class surveys, the majority said the writing improved their understanding of course content and that they had learned to draft essays; several indicated how much they enjoyed the assignments and the course overall.

In this general-education course, Parker and Mitchell did not offer domesticated college essays, but instead they contextualized the field report and the ethnology in numerous ways that gave students access to these genres as social and rhetorical practices. They linked the stated goals on the prompt to what they did with the genres during class. They built invention strategies directly into the writing assignment, which meant that students took detailed notes while they were in the field or as they were reading Shostak's book, the moves that experts make, before they drafted their papers. In both sections, Parker and Mitchell gave the students time to read each other's work, to consider what genres do for readers, and to discuss the rhetorical challenges anthropologists encounter when they write ethnology. Throughout the semester, Parker and Mitchell reflected on what they were doing, changing their approach to peer review for the second assignment, which also allowed Mitchell to discuss questions of stance directly with the students.

To write genres fluently, students have to find something to talk about. As they invent material, they have to learn how to manage the level of detail for readers, which involves ascertaining the motives for writing in the first place. And they also have to find the appropriate stance that, as we can see, is intimately linked to understanding the content. In all these ways, writers in college turn content into what their readers recognize as evidence. But, as I have stressed, for many writers achieving fluency in so many genres does not occur unless we can enhance how, where, and when they can talk and think about, practice, and receive feedback on "segments" of the whole practice. While they are immersed in the life of the social group that gives meaning to the practice, they surely benefit as well from explicitly discussing the rhetoric of genres. By building this context for genre, teachers can help students who would otherwise struggle or just would not find purpose in university writing to produce texts meaningful to both writer and reader.

# Conclusion

NICHOLAS GOLDBERG, a professor of psychology, supplied the title for our program's film, *Access to Learning*, when he remarked in his interview that through writing, his working-class students gain access to the skills and knowledge they can use to cross successfully into the professional world. Despite their varying expertise in foreign languages, international studies, biology, architecture, and mathematics, Goldberg's colleagues whom Christine Ballantine also interviewed shared his goal: all were dedicated to give their urban students better access to learning course content through writing. By way of closing, I briefly consider what access entails, for both teachers and students, in an institutional context.

In longitudinal research, some students express frustration because they believe their teachers block their access to genres. Most often, they blame unclear prompts or the lack of explicit guidelines and other supports for assignments (e.g., Herrington and Curtis). If professors do not make more explicit for their students the intellectual moves that genres embody, some writers tend to substitute the prompt for the genre. When experts read prompts, for instance, scientists who are writing grants, they tend to relate the prompt to other forms of discourse describing the task, such as models or what their peers say (Tardy). Scientists read a prompt recursively by participating in a rhetorical situation, just as, for instance, most academics write journal articles and books. By contrast, some students in psychology, cited in chapter 2, spent valuable time trying to crack the prompt's code in isolation instead of writing drafts or collecting information, not, we know from naturalistic study, an uncommon strategy. They tended to read the prompt in a linear manner, as if it provided the ingredients to a recipe, perhaps a strategy that the prompt invited. In her study of students who sought to decode prompts in this way, Theresa Lillis concludes that some writers in this situation believe they confront "an *institutional practice of mystery*" (127; original emphasis).

Similarly, many professors I have met at City and elsewhere or read about in published accounts of other programs believe that students must learn to solve the institutional practice of mystery. This is a principled viewpoint: some professors believe that solving the mystery fulfills a student's initiation to schooling; others, that it enables students to freely explore ideas without too much interruption from a teacher. Many professors subscribe to this apprenticeship model of learning based on their own experiences as novices in a field: they did not receive explicit guidance, but they figured out what their readers wanted and succeeded. From this perspective, writing vague prompts (or, not writing assignments down at all) poses a *necessary* rhetorical challenge for students to explore.

When I interviewed Andy Wheelock, who taught the successful media-communications course cited in chapter 3, he explained that WAC challenged his ingrained belief in this model of learning. His approach to teaching writing, he said, was shaped by his apprenticeship, first as a student at an Ivy League university and later as an executive in the New York City advertising industry: "I just figured it out as I went along." Before working with the fellow, "I thought, let the students work with the [prompt], and then they'll figure it out." In the introduction, I noted that genre knowledge is so tacit that experts are not aware of how they learned the rhetoric of their fields. As Wendy Strachan concludes, "For all of the faculty interviewed [at Simon Fraser University], it seemed that the process of the acquisition of their particular disciplinary discourse was so embedded in their apprenticeship in the discipline that it was invisible to them" (142).

Lave and Wenger's apprenticeship model is powerful because it shows how the writing of genres occurs through social interaction. It reveals how and why a novice needs access to a situation in order to acquire a complex genre. But even Lave and Wenger concede that old-timers can deliberately block newcomers from direct access to a practice. Professors who lament the quality of writing they receive but do not return papers regularly with feedback may be willfully blocking students' access to an institutional practice. More unwittingly, we also block access if we do not attempt to clarify our expectations on a prompt and provide more support and guidelines for the writing we assign. The CUNY fellows who lacked expertise in WAC learned through immersion but also through some systematic reflection on what they were doing. Yet, some scholars believe that students will pick up required genres by completing the coursework, arguing that if they acquire special field languages, they will also acquire the genres that embody those languages.

We need more research on this question because some evidence casts doubt on whether apprenticeships really do allow the novice to pick up important genres, either as medical students on the job (Lingard and Haber) or through absorbing the content of a class (Beaufort; Carter, Ferzli, and Wiebe). Research on the problem of transferring writing skills across situations suggests that even when a student does successfully produce a required genre, he or she may have scant rhetorical awareness of why he or she succeeded or of what writing does in a discipline (Beaufort; Greene, "Question of Authenticity"; Wardle, "Understanding 'Transfer' from FYC"). Also important in the context of institutional access, some research cited in the introduction indicates that students may not transfer their knowledge from composition classes across situations because professors do not provide the opportunity for them to do so. If we teach intense revision habits typical of some university experts, but our colleagues do not build drafts into a syllabus and explicitly discuss revision's importance, then the opportunity for transfer is, indeed, lost. Unsurprisingly, students will assume that the situation of a composition course is so narrow its skills like revision do not apply in new situations.

Some theorists, especially those influenced by the new rhetoric, spurn direct instruction in writing because they proceed from apprenticeship models; equally, though, some WAC specialists immersed in the tenets of writing-to-learn sometimes reject the role that overt instruction plays. Yet, we should consider how teachers contextualize any writing instruction they provide. In our program, students rejected workshops where fellows taught skills without reference to the course content or major assignments. This included, for example, a workshop on using topic sentences in paragraphs a fellow gave to students enrolled in an architectural-history class. But, I referred to Wheelock's media-communications class where students thought they understood how the conventional thesis statement applied to their specific situation after receiving some overt instruction from their professor. I also showed how Julia Mitchell explicitly taught Cassandra Parker's students to organize their notes into a comparative field report. The students said this workshop was very helpful, and the outside readers who rated their work thought the essays were well organized. It is not productive to talk about forms in isolation, but in this case, Mitchell described organization in the context of the students' notes and the comparative structures typical of anthropological ways of doing. Giving skills flesh and bone in this way turns "conventions" into meaningful rhetorical craft and opens up one pathway to a genre.

Often, those professors who are willing to join WAC programs are ready to challenge uncomplicated apprenticeship models. They sometimes come to WAC and other faculty-development programs because they want to provide their students with more explicit access to the tools of their fields, of which written genres is only one. The partners with whom we worked most successfully challenged habitual approaches towards teaching and learning, and this is probably why they were willing to share expertise with PhD students in the first place. Most believed that their deliberate choices as teachers could matter: learning by trial and error was not enough. In his application for a fellow, a professor from the School of Architecture wrote, "The objective here would be to set a clear path for students' success, rather than just setting high standards and hoping they reach these." Concerned professors like these made explicitly time-consuming efforts to clear a path for their students towards required forms: they spent considerable time talking to fellows and to me;

they revised and shared their materials; they considered new assignments, attended workshops, experimented with technology, or made contact with support services like the Writing Center.

These individual efforts were always constrained by what the institution provided. This is a short way of saying that it is not just teachers who provide explicit access to genres—institutions do, too. Genres have socializing power, so it makes sense that individuals can improve their teaching of genres by talking to other people about rhetoric in general and the rhetoric of their fields in particular. The CUNY Writing Fellows Program, sponsored by CUNY's Office of Academic Affairs, is a complex administrative and expensive pedagogical effort, but on many campuses, the fellows sparked new faculty development and WAC programs. Queens, Lehman, and York colleges, Hostos, Kingsborough, and LaGuardia community colleges have all established robust WAC programs, and for some years at least, the monthly meetings held with WAC coordinators resulted in particularly rich debates about teaching and learning across individual institutions. This book is just one small consequence of CUNY's decision to establish and then fund a structure that provided professors with additional direct access to WAC programs.

At CUNY (as at other institutions), the overall picture of access is complex and shifting for faculty and students alike. When CUNY abolished remedial programs at the senior colleges, the board also created WAC. At the same time, in the past few years, CUNY has consistently raised admissions standards at the senior colleges and shifted the burden of English proficiency testing to community colleges. Meanwhile, CUNY increased demands for professors to produce more scholarship on all the campuses without reducing course loads. This type of pressure means that it is more challenging for professors to devote their attention to those aspects of teaching writing that will most affect students' access to genre: talking with colleagues, frequent response to writing, or one-to-one conferences during office hours. Within and beyond CUNY, large class size remains a chief obstacle for WAC programs.

Institutions must commit to give all students but especially those who lack significant social experience with university expectations full access to academic genres by creating the conditions where faculty can teach, and students learn, to read and write better than they do. It is a collective decision whether institutions reduce class size or provide students and their teachers with access to technology and writing centers. Similarly, it is a collective decision whether institutions decide to reward improved teaching and maintain faculty development efforts that give professors access to conversations about teaching and learning.

A more deliberate approach to teaching genre as a social action can enhance how well our students write about special information. To do this, we have to be willing in the first place to believe that we can find "a clear path" to genres rather than just "hoping" students grope (or expecting them to grope) toward it through trial and error. We have to be willing to examine a dominant model of how we learn and how we teach and to ask how much this model relies on asking (or expecting) students to solve institutional mysteries. We have to be willing to examine those questions that genre research raises: the extent of general writing ability and the nature of our own rhetorical expertise. But, professors cannot do all this alone: ultimately, it is institutions that will decide whether and how much to support the rich efforts at teaching and learning described in this book. Together, professors and institutions can assure that students of all kinds, who speak many tongues and come from many places, may participate more fully and more *pleasurably* in the making of everyday university genres.

**APPENDIXES**

**WORKS CITED**

**INDEX**

Field Projects: Professor Cassandra Parker

### INTRODUCTION: THE ASSIGNMENTS

1. The Congo Project, based upon your observations of the gorilla exhibit at the Bronx Zoo

2. The *Nisa* Project, based upon your reading of Shostak's ethnography *Nisa*

One of the most valuable insights anthropology affords is the ability to see the "ordinary" in completely new ways. Each of the assignments described on the following pages allows you to do this but through different techniques. The Congo Project allows you to compare human behavior to that of another species altogether, while the *Nisa* Project asks you to compare your own modern-day culture to that of another contemporary society with quite different cultural practices. In each case, you are likely to observe both commonalities and differences between the "other" you are observing and the culture with which you are most familiar—your own. As a result of this comparison, you will be able to see what is most familiar to you with a fresh perspective, whether you are riding the subway, interacting with your family and friends, walking through the park, or taking a course at City College.

### GENERAL GUIDELINES

Each project is broken down into three stages of writing: note taking, first draft, and final draft. Attached to each project description, you will find a note-taking guide to be used during the observational stages of the assignment (i.e., reading *Nisa* or visiting the gorilla exhibit). These sheets may be filled out by hand—neatly, as you will be exchanging them with other students as the basis for class discussion. You will then use these notes to compose a first draft of your paper, which should be typed and double spaced. After editing and revision, each of these projects will result in a five-to-ten-page final draft, which should also be typed and double spaced.

Your final papers will be graded according to three criteria: *content*, which refers to the comprehensiveness, appropriateness, and accuracy of the ideas and factual information presented in the report; *organization*, which refers to how the ideas and information are developed and presented; and *presentation*, which refers to grammar, spelling, and appropriateness of the report's presentation.

## Congo Project

Objective: The point of this project is to make inferences about gorilla behavior based upon your observations of one of the groups of gorillas on display at the Congo exhibit at the Bronx Zoo and to compare your findings to what you observe in human behavior.

Process: Observe one group of gorillas for a half hour, and record what you see in note form. Using the guidelines on the following page, take three sets of notes, pertaining to (a) the setting in which you are making the observations, (b) the relative positions in the troop of the individuals you are observing, and (c) the behavior of the gorillas. Be sure to pay attention to the labels provided by the exhibit, which identify individuals by name and explain their position in the group as well as their relationship to other gorillas in the exhibit. Next, take half an hour to observe the humans at the exhibit. Note any similarities between gorilla social structure/behavior and that of the humans you observe, using the same three categories as you did for the gorillas.

Outline: Introduction: Begin by using your notes in section (a) to give your reader a general description of the observational setting for both groups observed.

Body: The bulk of your report should be devoted to describing your observations of the gorillas, relying on the notes you took in sections (b) and (c) of the guide. Compare your observations of the gorillas to what you

observed in human behavior. Did you observe any
behaviors among the gorillas that you also observed
among the humans? Do their respective social structures bear any resemblance to each other?

Conclusion: Discuss any broad comparisons/contrasts
you discovered between these two types of primates.
In what ways are modern humans like gorillas, and in
what ways do we differ?

## *Nisa* Project

Objective: In this project, you will write an ethnology comparing
aspects of !Kung life, as described in Shostak's *Nisa*, with
those of your own culture—however you define it.

Process: Before you begin reading, go over the list of topics
listed on the note-taking guideline. This will help you
to read more efficiently and with purpose. As you are
reading the text, be sure to take notes not only on what
you learn of the !Kung but also on your observations
of similar processes or situations in your own cultural
setting. What rings familiar, and how do the !Kung
handle things differently?

Outline: Introduction: Take several sentences to discuss what
you plan to write about and why it is important. Your
introduction should give the reader a general sense of
what to expect from the body of the paper. Be sure to
mention the topics you will discuss and to define your
own culture here.

Body: In this section, choose three aspects of culture
that *Nisa* discusses for the !Kung, and compare them to
similar aspects in your own culture. You will find some
relevant topics on the following note-taking sheet, but
you should also feel free to discuss other appropriate
topics that interest you.

Conclusion: Discuss what you liked and did not like
about the book. What was done well, and what could
have been improved—in terms of both the content of
the book and the style in which it was written?

CONGO PROJECT

## Notes: Gorillas
*Observational setting*

Note the kind of gorillas you are observing, where they come from, their habitat both in the wild and at the zoo, the weather, the time of day, and which troop you are observing.

*Positions*

Sort the animals out by their positions in the troop—infants, juveniles, adult male, adult females, dominant males, and the like, using the identifying labels provided by the exhibit as a guide.

*Behavior*

Record what the gorillas are doing. Are the adults doing different things from the juveniles? Which one is spending time with which one? Note particularly any behavior that you infer is related to the fact that the gorillas are in a zoo and not in the wild.

## Notes: Humans
*Observational setting*

Now take some time to observe the humans who are visiting the exhibit. As you did with the gorillas, make notes on the overall setting: what social functions does this space perform for the humans who are there?

*Positions*

Take some notes on the positions of the various humans around you. Sort them, as best you can, into categories such as sex, gender, age, class, ethnicity, and the like. Do you observe any commonalities between human social structure and that of the gorillas?

*Behavior*

Record what the humans are doing. Are the adults doing different things from the juveniles? Who is spending time with whom? How does the behavior you observe relate to the setting in which you are observing? Do you observe any behaviors common to humans and gorillas?

## In-class Exercise: Mapping a Field Report

*Introduction*

Now that you have made your observations of gorillas and humans, it is time to turn your raw data into the rough draft of a narrative that will convey what you learned to your reader. In constructing this text, you will have to make some choices regarding your organization of the material. This exercise is designed to help you organize your thoughts into a coherent structure that presents your findings in a clear, accessible field report. In a sense, your objective in this exercise is to "map out" the text of your essay in order to begin to shape the details contained in your notes into a more structured text.

*Purpose*

Since the nature of this assignment is essentially comparative, your task is not only to describe the observational setting, social positions, and behavior of both gorillas and humans but also to draw some general conclusions about the ways in which the two groups are similar and the ways in which they are different. The two models provided below offer different ways to do both: to provide a description of each group and to elaborate that description with a comparative analysis of the two. Model 1 allows you to integrate description and analysis, while model 2 allows you to separate the two tasks into different sections.

*Note*

The models provided in this exercise are just that: models. You should of course feel free to organize your essay differently if you like. When you have completed your rough draft, you may choose to leave the subtitles in the text (or use subtitles of your own) or take them out altogether and instead present your essay as one flowing narrative. Their purpose at this time is to help you move from the note-taking stage to the draft-writing stage in an organized fashion.

*Exercise*

Using one of the models below—or using one of your own—take half an hour to begin "filling in" the sections of your rough draft. You may write in complete sentences or simply jot down some ideas you intend to address in each section. Whichever model you choose to use, it is not necessary to write "in order" (beginning with the introduction and following with each of the other sections in turn). Many writers find it helpful to write the body of the paper first and then go back and write the introduction later. In fact, working through the main text may give you a better understanding of the general argument you'd like to make, which you can then state later on when you write the introduction.

Once you have completed this exercise—and you may continue working on it outside the classroom—your next step will be to transfer your written work on these sheets into a word-processing program so that you can complete your rough draft, print it, and bring it to class. Once you have constructed the first draft, we will move on to a peer-review exercise which will allow you to work on issues of vocabulary, grammar, clarity, and so forth.

*NISA* **PROJECT**

**Notes**

| Behavior | !Kung | Your Culture |
|---|---|---|
| Economic Life | | |
| Marriage | | |
| Children | | |
| Death | | |
| Gender | | |
| Healing & Spirituality | | |
| Aging | | |
| Other | | |

## THINKING ABOUT CULTURE

## Note to Fellows/Faculty Using This Exercise

The "introductory points" section of this exercise was not presented to the class on paper, as it is here, but comprised an open class discussion in which students were invited to participate. Rather than simply present these issues to the class, the objective is to lead them through it via specific examples, questions, and discussion. The overall purpose of the exercise is to get them to think about the concept of "culture" in a more complex way than it is presented in most anthropological textbooks, including the one used for this course (Haviland's *Anthropology*). The freewrite and notes from the introductory discussion can then be used as a basis for writing about culture (in this course, for the essay assignment on the ethnography *Nisa: Life of a !Kung Woman*).

## Introductory Points

1. The textbook for this course defines culture as "the abstract values, beliefs, and perceptions of the world that lie behind people's behavior (and that are) shared by members of a society" (381). (Ask for examples of shared cultural values, beliefs, or perceptions from the class.)

2. One example of a shared, collective cultural value often cited by anthropologists is that of personal space. All human beings appear to have established notions of appropriate personal space under different social circumstances and will instinctively move to correct a situation in which that value has been violated (for instance, most people will move away from someone who is standing too close to them for comfort). This value differs cross-culturally. (This can be demonstrated physically in the classroom.)

3. However, there are many situations in which the above definition simply does not work. (Ask the students to recognize problems with the textbook definition.)

A. For one thing, the textbook definition does not take into account the possibility of cultural conflict. What happens when members of a society do not agree upon the content of those values, beliefs and perceptions that are supposedly shared by all?

B. For another, it does not question who within a given society has the authority to define that cultural content. The definition lacks any sense of social, political, or economic power and appears to posit culture as a benign, even beneficent, force in people's lives. How can it account for the possibility of culture as a conservative oppression as well?

C. And what is important, it does not take into account the existence of cultural change. Yet we know that cultural change not only takes place but appears to be far more prevalent than cultural "stability." How do values, behaviors, and perceptions change over time if culture is some shared, eternal essence?

4. Such questions come into particularly sharp focus when the values, beliefs, and perceptions of different cultures clash in the process of contact, conquest, and imperialist expansion. A classic example might be that of Western feminism (by its very nature a universalist politics) clashing with patriarchal cultural practices. Historically, such clashes between universal worldviews (feminism versus patriarchy) have produced conflict not only between societies but also within them and, in conjunction with political-economic change, have engendered internal cultural revolutions that belie the textbook definition of culture as "shared."

5. The textbook definition of culture, embraced by many early anthropologists, gives rise to the idea of cultural relativism: the notion that different cultural practices are equally valid regardless of their differences in content. While historically useful in the context of combating Euro-American ethnocentrism, cultural relativism has presented the same problems as the textbook definition of culture when used to defend such practices as racism or genocide. What happens to the notion of universal human rights (or any other universal value) if all cultural practices are equal? (Ask the class for historically examples of such conflicts: the classic case against extreme relativism is Nazism.)

6. In conclusion, anthropologists have found culture in practice to be a far more complex problematic than textbook definitions would allow. Thinking of culture as a *process,* inherently imbued with conflict, change, and struggle, rather than an unchanging *product,* brings the notion of culture close to historical reality.

## Exercise

Ask students to think of a specific situation in which the found themselves at odds with their own "culture," however they define that. Mention gender, sexual identity, race, ethnicity, religion, class, kinship, and language as possible bases for culture conflict. Have them freewrite on this topic for ten to fifteen minutes, then divide the class into discussion groups to compare notes, taking another fifteen minutes for group discussion. Fellows and the professor(s) should circulate around the room, listening and participating. Then bring the class back together for general discussion, focusing on how this exercise might help them to think about the particular writing assignment in question (in this case, we had asked students to compare three aspects of culture from "their own" culture with those they found in the *Nisa* ethnography.)

## Contextual Note

This exercise works particularly well at City College because of the diversity of the student body. Fellows should be prepared to discuss the idea of living in two or more cultures simultaneously, since many students (or their parents) come to New York from different geographical, linguistic, and cultural backgrounds (for instance, in a two-section course of roughly fifty students, we counted twenty-three different languages spoken by the students). Fellows and faculty should be prepared to spontaneously use this diversity to foster a creative, complex discussion.

## Help for Nonanthropologists

For fellows or faculty seeking background literature on a more complex concept of "culture" in preparation for this exercise, the following readings may be useful:

Roseberry, William. "Balinese Cockfights and the Seduction of Anthropology." *Anthropologies and Histories: Essays in Culture, History, and Political Economy.* New Brunswick: Rutgers UP, 1991. 17–29.

Wolf, Eric. Introduction. *Europe and the People without History.* Berkeley: U of California P, 1982. 3–24.

### PEER-REVIEW EXERCISE: *NISA* DRAFTS

## Note to Fellows/Faculty by Julia Mitchell

Cassandra Parker and I designed this peer-review exercise in response to midsemester student surveys requesting (a) more classwide discussion and (b) less paperwork in the peer-review process. After reading the first drafts of the *Nisa* essay, we chose one "model" paper to be presented as part of a peer-review that would be done with the class as a whole and based upon reading and open discussion rather than written responses, as opposed to the first peer-review project we conducted. We then asked the permission of the student who wrote the draft, who graciously allowed us to use it in both sections of the course. We photocopied the draft onto transparency paper and had the students read it collectively on an overhead projector rather than making paper copies for everyone.

## Process

Take fifteen minutes to read the paper as a class. Once the initial reading is complete, open the floor for discussion, beginning with how students felt about the paper, and moving on to issues of structure, organization, tone, detail, examples, transitions, and so forth. The overall purpose is to generate discussion as to why this text is a good paper and therefore open a window on the question of what makes for good writing in anthropology or, more specifically, what makes for a good comparative ethnography. Close the session with a brief discussion on how the text could be improved and edited into a final draft. The discussion should generate a list of successful writing techniques that students might apply to their own papers, which can be mapped out on the blackboard.

## Results

This exercise was somewhat experimental. Our goal was to get the students to talk about writing in a less-structured way than we had attempted before. The exercise was loosely based on a class-wide, open-ended peer review conducted in [an interdisciplinary seminar she worked in the previous semester]. The results were oddly mixed. In the morning section of the course, the students actively and enthusiastically participated in the discussion, and we were able to come up with a "map" on the chalkboard of key aspects of the sample text that made it a readable, interesting paper. The students were also able to successfully abstract from this particular piece to ethnographic writing in general, which led to a discussion of the postmodern turn in anthropology, including issues of anthropological authority and cultural conflict discussed in a previous exercise. In the afternoon section, students were far less willing to participate (as they had typically been all semester) and required far more structured (even leading) questions about the text. Ironically, the afternoon exercise eventually led to a discussion of the gaps, problems, and silences in the ethnography *Nisa*, which students were assigned to compare with their own cultural backgrounds.

## Lessons

I continue to believe that classwide peer reviews can be useful, particularly when used in conjunction with more specific, one-on-one peer reviews that ask students to exchange papers with a colleague and give specific written comments. Their primary value lies in demonstrating *how* to go about doing a peer review in the first place, because they allow the class to *discover* specific textual issues to focus on (such as essay organization, topical transitions, or use of detail) rather than simply being *instructed* on what to look for. In retrospect, I believe this exercise may have worked better using both paper copies for each student and the overhead projector for general discussion. It may also help to ask students to read the essay ahead of time.

## Left-hand Column

1. When you watch the video, focus on one or more children's behaviors. Observe closely what he or she does.

2. Write in this column what you have just observed. Focus on exactly what the child did and said. Avoid opinionated statements ("She is so adorable," "He must be spoiled," and the like).

*Example from a student log, left-hand column*

During a music lesson, a student named Isury and Jacob had a confrontation. Jacob had two bells in his hand, and he wanted Isury's instrument so he hit her on the head accidentally while trying to take her instrument. Instantly, Isury turned around and said, "Why did you hit me, Jacob?" Jacob then grabbed her instrument and started to play. Isury then started to cry, and Jacob started to laugh.

## Right-hand Column (Assignment Due September 27)

3. Think about developmental theories you have learned so far (consult assigned readings and lecture notes). Does the behavior of the child you have just observed illustrate or contradict some theories?

4. Write down relevant theories (add a brief explanation of the theories; add page numbers from the readings) and how these theories relate to your observation. (There is no one right answer in this activity; explore.)

*Example from a student log, right-hand column*

*Aggression and hostility in young children.* I believe this article applies to this situation so much. For instance, this article explains a situation where a child pushed another child down in her eagerness to obtain a toy, causing the other child to cry; did she "intend" to hurt the pushed down child or merely to get the toy? Instrumental aggression; hostile aggression (335–440).

## APPENDIX 3: MUSIC-APPRECIATION CLASS

Attend a classical concert at a major NYC concert hall, and write a review.

### Prewriting Strategies

Read a music review in the *New York Times*.
Think about these reviews before you go to the performance and listen to the CD.
What sorts of things did the reviewer make note of?
What elements did he or she talk about?
Why is the piece considered important?
What does your professor want you to listen for?
Make notes as ideas occur to you.

### At the Concert

Listen quietly, and enjoy the concert.
As you listen, keep in mind what you learned from the text and from classroom discussions, such as, movement, instruments/vocalists in unison (rhythmic and melodic), general contour of melodic phrases, tempo changes, instruments being played, and the like.
Place the music in its proper context, such as, period, genre.
Cue in for behavior from the people around you.
Take notes at intermission (it is distracting to write during the concert).
Keep your concert ticket and program.
Compare mentally the live performance with what you thought it would be like before you went to the concert.

### Writing the Review Paper

Have you defined a thesis from your observations and analysis?
How is the music organized?

What unifies the music?

What style is the music and from what period?

Have you structured your paper so that it is logical and persuasive?

Have your checked your sentence structure, grammar, and punctuation?

Have you incorporated words from our classroom discussions and music vocabulary/lexicon?

Is your paper interesting?

## Ask the When, Where, Why, What, and Who of the Music and Performance

When—Does the music sound like it comes from a particular time?

Is it your time?

Where—Does the music sound like it comes from a particular place?

Is it your place?

Why—Does this music have a purpose?

Is it for dancing or for listening?

Is it religious or secular?

What—What is the medium?

Is it being sung and/or played?

Is it a solo or an ensemble piece?

Is it excited or calm?

Is it intimate or monumental?

Is it expository or developmental?

Does it have one continuous mood, or does it have contrasting sections?

Is it narrative (it has a program or story), or is it abstract?

Who—What do you know about the composer?

What do you know about the performer(s)?

What do you know about the audience?

Last, but not least, we need to find out

How—How is the music coming to you and under what circumstances?

## RUBRIC FOR SCORING CONCERT REVIEWS

A score of 6 is a superb concert review. The writer offers an overall evaluation of the quality of the concert. The writer provides a thorough, well-organized overview of the musical performance and provides a distinct context for the concert. The writer's use of musical terminology shows a firm grasp of basic concepts in an introductory course. The writer integrates information about the experience of the concert or music history smoothly into the paper. The essay is a pleasure to read, with few sentence-level errors.

A score of 5 is an above-average review. The writer offers some evaluation of the quality of the concert. The writer provides a well-organized overview of the musical performance and provides a distinct context for the concert. The writer uses musical terminology appropriately. While the writer provides information about the experience of the concert or music history, he or she may not always integrate this information smoothly into the paper. The essay is easy to read and has few grammatical errors.

A score of 4 is a slightly above average concert review. The writer does not provide a clear evaluation of the quality of the concert but does offer a well-organized overview of the musical performance. The writer provides some context for the concert and uses musical terminology adequately. The writer offers some information about the experience of the concert or music history but does not integrate this information smoothly into the overall review. The essay is easy to read. Grammatical errors may be present but do not hinder the reader's understanding.

A score of 3 is an average concert review. The writer does not provide a clear evaluation of the quality of the concert. The writer provides some context for the concert and offers an adequately organized overview of the musical performance. Though he or she may use musical terminology, he or she does so awkwardly or inappropriately. The writer offers some information about the experience of the concert or music history but does not integrate the information smoothly into the paper. The essay is less of a pleasure to read than other essays. Grammatical errors may be present but do not seriously hinder the reader's understanding.

A score of 2 is a slightly below average concert review. The writer does not provide an evaluation of the quality of the concert and provides little context for the concert. The concert review may not be clearly organized. The writer may use some musical terminology but does so inappropriately. The writer includes information about the experience of the concert or the history of music, but this information may not be used appropriately. The essay may be difficult to read. Grammatical errors may hinder the reader's understanding.

A score of 1 is a poor concert review. The writer does not provide an evaluation of the quality of the concert and provides no context for the concert. The writer does not use musical terminology accurately. The writer does not organize the material clearly. The writer offers little of the experience of the concert or the history of music. The essay is not a pleasure to read or may be very difficult to read. Grammatical errors may hinder the reader's understanding.

## Preliminary Art-viewing Assignment

*Goals of paper 1*

This preliminary art-viewing assignment is designed to help you prepare for the first formal paper that you will write for this class (due March 18)—called "Paper 1" on your syllabus.

For paper 1, you will write a philosophical assessment of an artwork that you see and acutely observe on March 4. The paper requires you to observe a work in thorough detail and then to assess it in terms of either Kant's or Plato's ideas about beauty.

In order to write paper 1, you will need to craft a detailed description of the work of art you choose to observe while on the Chelsea gallery tour and make a judgment about whether Kant or Plato would consider the object you have chosen to be "beautiful." You will also need to interrogate claims Kant or Plato makes about the condition of something being beautiful.

*Preparing for paper 1 through a low-stakes art-viewing assignment*

The following preliminary writing assignment for art-viewing prepares you for the demands of paper 1 by requiring you to (1) write a very detailed description of the work of art you choose to observe, (2) practice skills of philosophical inquiry by asking you to make a personal aesthetic judgment, in deeming the work beautiful or not beautiful, (3) interrogate your own standards of beauty, and (4) make a general claim about what can be called "beautiful," as Kant and Plato do.

### Viewing

Choose one work or a small set of related works (a series; several pieces by a single artist) that will be the subject of your preliminary art-viewing assignment and then subsequently also the subject of paper 1.

Walk around the piece or stand in front of it, and take notes. It is very important to take detailed notes; thorough notes will make the task of describing the work of art in your preliminary paper and paper 1 much easier. Ask yourself, for example:

What materials is the piece made of?
Is it representational or not?
How would you describe its shape, its colors, its textures?
Is it symmetrical? How does the light hit it?
What mood does the piece convey? Or does it convey no mood at all?

Write down some notes about your own feelings about the piece. Do you find it beautiful? Why or why not? Do you think beauty is a relevant category to consider when apprehending a work of art?

## To Consider before Writing

At home before writing, think about any connections between your views about the artwork and your conception of beauty. What do your views say about the conditions that something must meet before you judge it to be beautiful?

Use your description of the work of art to make a general statement of your view on the preconditions that must be met for you to consider something "beautiful."

## Writing

Write a two-page statement that begins with a description of the artwork you have chosen to observe. Include your own opinion about the work, and then articulate and support the claims upon which your opinion is based. In closing, address the issue of whether or not you think the question of beauty is relevant to art.

### CRITICAL READING THROUGH ANNOTATION

## Assignment 1

*Annotation as a critical-reading strategy*

This week, you are reading some sections of Kant's *Critique of Judgment*. Philosophical readings tend to be dense and complex; they require careful reading and interrogation. When you read, you are entering into a dialogue with the text. Reading is an act of interpretation. In order to do a critical reading of a philosophical text—or, for that matter, any other complicated text—it's a good idea to think and write your way through a text *as you read* in order to make sure that you understand what the author is trying to communicate and can interrogate any claims the author makes. One important critical reading strategy is to *annotate* what you are reading. Annotation can involve circling important phrases, underlining key sentences, and taking notes in the margins of the text. Such notes might include rephrasing of the author's language in your own words, raising questions, defining words when necessary, jotting down doubts, criticisms, or hypothetical examples, making observations about the tone, attitude, style, or structure of the text; and even drawings or diagrams.

*The annotation assignment*

This annotation exercise is designed to help you critically engage Kant's text. You will receive an annotation model—an excerpt from a complicated text by the sociologist, Pierre Bourdieu—as well as an unannotated excerpt from the assigned Kant reading.

1. Observe how the annotated model documents the process of reading/engaging the text. There are notes in the margins, examples to illustrate points, questions raised, and definitions of words. Key sections are underlined and words are circled.

2. Now, annotate the Kant model you have received. Write in the margins of the Kant excerpt thoughts, clarifications, disagreements, examples, or questions you have as you read. You may also define terms, draw diagrams, and circle and underline key phrases or passages. Be careful to make clear what section of the text your notes refer to by drawing an arrow or some other indicator. You will turn in this annotated Kant excerpt to the professor on February 26th.

USING MODELS TO TEACH SCIENTIFIC WRITING

Read through the model-methods sections quickly to get an overall idea of what they say. Then, read through more slowly as you answer the following questions in writing:

1. What is the purpose of the methods section of a scientific paper?

2. What is described in the first paragraph of the methods section of this paper? Baseline (pre-measurement) set up.

3. What are the important elements to include in the methods section? Underline or circle these in the papers. Next to what you underlined, write a brief explanation (a word or phrase) identifying what you underlined, for example, "dependent variable."

**Examples of items that might be the elements**

Rationale for experimental design
Equipment setup
Baseline conditions
Dependent variable
Independent variable
Control variable
Calculations

4. What is the structure of the methods section?

Baseline setup
  —including equipment ("home" tanks for fish), independent variable (temperature), object of study (bass)
Dependent variable
How equipment was set up
How equipment functioned
Process of taking measurement of DV

How DV was calculated
Rationale for how experiment was designed
Measurement of control variables

5. What would you change or improve in these methods sections, and why?

## Sample Methods Sections

*Sample 1*

> The first step is to decide amongst the group which individual is going to consume the 1,000 ml of distilled water, 100 g of glucose in 400 ml of water, and the 100 g of glucose in 200 ml of water. After making this decision, consume the solution of your choice for 30 minutes. When the 30 minutes' waiting period is up, each individual needs to obtain a specimen cup and go collect their first urine specimen. The next step is to record the total volume of urine specimen (which can be read directly from the specimen cup) in the table. Divide the total volume of urine specimen by the number of minutes (which would be 30) since the bladder was last emptied, to arrive at the urinary flow rate in ml/min. To find the specific gravity, drop two to three drops of urine in the glass of the Refractometer with a disposable dropper. Close the lid, and wait for 30 seconds before holding the Refractometer's main prism towards light. A circular field with graduations down the center will be seen, with the upper portion of the field being blue and the lower portion being white; take the reading of the line that divides both portions. Lastly, to test for the urinary glucose (dependent variable), take a glucose test strip, and dip it into the urine. Wait for 30 seconds, and then compare the reagent side of the test area with the color chart. Repeat the above steps for the remaining one and a half hours.

*Sample 2*

We began the experiment by connecting the CI-6534A Low Pressure Sensor (0–10 kPa) to Data Studio Science workshop 500 interface, which is connected to a Dell computer containing the Data Studio Science program. Using a single-edged razor blade, we cut a stem 2–3 cm above the soil from Draceana 8 Sanderiana. We immersed the stem in a bowl of fresh water. We shaved the fresh-cut end of the stem to a 45-degree angle, keeping the edge submerged in the water; a ring of petroleum jelly was smeared 4 cm above the cut. Gwendolyn in the meantime connected the quick-release connector to the plastic tubing with an adaptor to fit our plant. Using a pipette, she instilled water leaving a 2 cm air gap between the water and the end with the quick-release connector. We connected the other end with the plant, inserting the previously cut stem end into the tubing. The quick-release connector was attached to CI-6534A Low Pressure Sensor (0–10 kPa). Using clamps, base, and support rod (ME-9355), we maintained the plant and sensor upright. Using a light probe meter, we measured the room light intensity at 744 fc, and we ran our first measurement for ten minutes. We then adjusted a dual-headed lamp at the plant's side and took readings at the adjusted light readings of 2373 fc, 7570 fc, 31990 fc, and 34820 fc for ten minutes each. The dial on the dual light was adjusted spatially. The knob was divided into four, and the light intensities at these settings are as reported.

*Sample 3*

Click the setup button on the Data Studio Program, and the Pasco Interface will be displayed on the screen. Click on the icon representing the oxygen electrode, and place the oxygen electrode on the cover of the measuring jar.

The icon opened the Dissolved-Oxygen Sensor Properties box. We clicked the tab that said "Calibration." There was a display of the current reading in volts on the left and two boxes for high-point and low-point readings. Low point was set to 0.00 mg/1 and voltage set to 0.00. To find the high-point value, we referred to the table of "Concentration (mg/L) of Dissolved Oxygen at Saturation by Temperature and Barometric Pressure." The table showed the value of dissolved oxygen in saturated water at the temperature and barometric pressure at which measurements are being made today. After calibrating phase I, the experiment was started.

## APPENDIX 6: WRITING-TO-LEARN IN ART 100

(Excerpted from Henriksen, Linton, McCormack, Rome, Wallace, and Soliday, *Innovative Teaching at City College* 8–9)

### EXERCISE ACCOMPANIES TRANSCRIPT
### OF STUDENTS' GROUP DISCUSSION

*Context.* The instructor in an Art 100 course explained to the writing fellows that, too often, students did not now how to begin his assignment, which asks for an analysis and comparison of two different paintings from the Metropolitan Museum of Art. The instructor also explained that while some of the better papers managed to do a close analysis of the paintings, the weaker papers failed to use the vocabulary and concepts of art analysis that he had stressed in class.

To address these issues simultaneously, the writing fellows designed a collaborative in-class activity that asked the students to write about and discuss a variety of model openings for the assignment. *As is usually the case, the forum for writing and discussion enabled students to work with course content as well.* While writing about the variety of openings we provided, students practiced their use of art vocabulary and syntax. In addition, by discussing a variety of viewpoints about the paintings, they improved their analytical skills. *We know this because, with their permission, we taped the students' small-group discussions.* Transcripts of these tapes showed students using art terminology and concepts while they discussed the various paper openings (see *Evaluation* transcript, 34). *This exercise was not just about helping students learn how to write a good opening; it also increased the depth of their knowledge about course content.*

This exercise was developed as a revision exercise (the students had already written a draft) but can be modified for use early in the writing process as a way to focus ideas.

### IN-CLASS EXERCISE FOR ART 100
### Directions for the Instructor
*Background*
(Instructors may want to discuss this with their students prior to the start of the exercise.)

Many students have trouble beginning an essay. Usually, the two problems when students report this difficulty are: knowing how to start working on an assignment and knowing what constitutes a successful introduction to an essay. This exercise only concerns the latter case.

When students have difficulty writing an opening, they may not understand that different types of introductions are appropriate (advantageous) for different types of assignments. The students may simply not have a variety of openings in their arsenal. This in-class exercise makes students aware of a variety of opening styles and emphasizes that students need to move away from one-size-fits-all openings.

More important, the opening of an essay is where writers present their main ideas. When writers think more about openings, they consider the content of their essays and how to present their information more cohesively.

For maximum benefit, students should *write down* their responses to each opening. The instructor should collect and compile the groups' advice on openings. The lists can be typed up as a "newsletter" and handed out in the next class. As a group, then, they will have written a fairly complete guide to composing good introductions.

### IN-CLASS EXERCISE ON OPENINGS (75 MINUTES)

### Directions to students (distributed to the students)

In groups of four, decide on assignments for each group member as follows: timekeeper (keeps track of time and keeps the group on task), referee (makes sure that all speak and listen and settles all disagreements), recorder (compiles a list of important things to remember about openings), and speaker (reports back to the class about what went on in the group).

*Step 1: Reading, writing, and discussion*

Sample openings for a specific assignment will be distributed to each group, one at a time. For each sample, follow these steps: Read the opening twice, and take notes (annotate) as you read. Then, each group member should write a reaction to each opening. (You may want to use the questions below to guide your reactions.)

(1) Sample opening 1. What do you think of the opening? Does it do what an opening needs to do?

(2) Sample opening 2. Judging from this opening, would you want to read this essay? What is the style of the opening (length of sentences, vocabulary choices, figures of speech)? What else did you notice about this opening as compared to the other one?

(3) Sample opening 3. Judging from this opening, what do you think the essay will be about? What does the author include in the opening? What does he or she leave out? What else did you notice about this opening as compared to the other two?

Each group member should read his or her reactions, out loud, referring specifically to the openings in question. Be sure the recorder takes notes during this discussion.

After you have discussed the openings, the referee should lead a discussion about the openings: Which opening is most successful? Why? The recorder should take additional notes during the discussion.

### Step 2: Constructing a list of hints

As a group, review the recorder's notes, and construct a list of ten pieces of advice about openings. The speaker from each group will choose three items from this list to share with the whole class. The list will then be collected.

### Step 3: Reflection

Each group member should write a response to these questions: What do I want to remember when I write an opening for this class? What do I want to remember about openings in general?

### Step 4: Revision

As an assignment for the next class, look back at your own essay opening. Using what you have discussed in your groups, write a new opening as part of your revision process. (This does not mean line edit or reword but write a completely new version.) Remember that an opening is not necessarily one paragraph. Of course, since you have a completed draft done, you have the advantage of knowing what the rest of their paper is about. Writing the opening last may be a good writing strategy.

## WORKS CITED

Ariail, Jennie, and Thomas G. Smith. "Concept Analysis: Using an Academic Nursing Genre for Writing Instruction in Nursing." *Rhetoric of Healthcare: Essays toward a New Disciplinary Inquiry.* Ed. Barbara Heifferon and Stuart Brown. Cresskill, NJ: Hampton, 2008. 243–63. Print.

Bakhtin, M. M. *Speech Genres and Other Late Essays.* Trans. Vern McGee. Ed. Caryl Emerson and Michael Holquist. Austin: U of Texas P, 1986. Print.

Bartholomae, David. "Inventing the University." *Perspectives on Literacy.* Ed. Eugene Kintgen, Barry Kroll, and Mike Rose. Carbondale: Southern Illinois UP, 1988. 273–85. Print.

Barton, Ellen. "Contrastive and Non-Contrastive Connectives: Metadiscourse Functions in Argumentation." *Written Communication* 12.2 (1995): 219–39. Print.

———. "Evidentials, Argumentation, and Epistemological Stance." *College English* 55.7 (1993): 745–69. Print.

Bawarshi, Anis. *Genre and the Invention of the Writer: Reconsidering the Place of Invention in Composition.* Logan: Utah State UP, 2003. Print.

Bazerman, Charles. *Shaping Written Knowledge: The Genre and Activity of the Experimental Article in Science.* Madison: U of Wisconsin P, 1988. Print.

———. "Systems of Genres and the Enactment of Social Intentions." Freedman and Medway, *Genre and the New Rhetoric* 79–101.

Bazerman, Charles, and David R. Russell, eds. *Writing Selves/Writing Societies: Research from Activity Perspectives.* Fort Collins, CO: WAC Clearinghouse, February 1, 2003. Web. <http://wac.colostate.edu/books/selves_societies/selves_societies.pdf>.

Bean, John. *Engaging Ideas: The Professor's Guide to Integrating Writing, Critical Thinking, and Active Learning in the Classroom.* San Francisco: Jossey, 2001. Print.

Beason, Larry. "Feedback and Revision in Writing across the Curriculum Classes." *Research in the Teaching of English* 27.4 (1993): 395–422. Print.

Beason, Larry, and Laurel Darrow. "Listening as Assessment: How Students and Teachers Evaluate WAC." Yancey and Huot 97–121.

Beaufort, Anne. *College Writing and Beyond: A New Framework for University Writing Instruction*. Logan: Utah State UP, 2007. Print.

Belcher, Diane. "Writing Critically across the Curriculum." Belcher and Braine 135–54.

Belcher, Diana, and George Braine, eds. *Academic Writing in a Second Language: Essays on Research and Pedagogy*. Norwood, NJ: Ablex, 1995. Print.

Bergmann, Linda, and Janet Zepernick. "Disciplinarity and Transfer: Students' Perceptions of Learning to Write." *WPA: Writing Program Administration* 31.1–2 (2007): 124–49. Print.

Berkenkotter, Carol, and Thomas Huckin. *Genre Knowledge in Disciplinary Communication: Cognition/Culture/Power*. Hillsdale, NJ: Erlbaum, 1995. Print.

Bhatia, Vijay. *Analysing Genre: Language Use in Professional Settings*. London: Longman, 1993. Print.

Brandt, Deborah. *Literacy as Involvement: The Acts of Writers, Readers, and Texts*. Carbondale: Southern Illinois UP, 1990. Print.

Brandt, Deborah, and Katie Clinton. "Limits of the Local: Expanding Perspectives on Literacy as a Social Practice." *Journal of Literacy Research* 34.3 (2002): 337–56. Print.

Broad, Bob. *What We Really Value: Beyond Rubrics in Teaching and Assessing Writing*. Logan: Utah State UP, 2003. Print.

Carroll, Lee Ann. *Rehearsing New Roles: How College Students Develop as Writers*. Carbondale: Southern Illinois UP, 2002. Print.

Carter, Michael. "Ways of Knowing, Doing, and Writing in the Disciplines." *College Composition and Communication* 58.3 (2007): 385–418. Print.

Carter, Michael, Miriam Ferzli, and Eric Wiebe. "Teaching Genre to English First—Language Adults: A Study of the Laboratory Report." *Research in the Teaching of English* 38.4 (2004): 395–419. Print.

Chiseri-Strater, Elizabeth. *Academic Literacies: The Public and Private Discourse of University Students*. Portsmouth, NH: Boynton, 1991. Print.

Christie, Frances, and J. R. Martin, eds. *Genre and Institutions: Social Processes in the Workplace and School*. 1997. London: Continuum, 2000. Print.

"City University of New York Board of Trustees Minutes of Proceedings." January 25, 1999. TS. Print. "Writing across the Curriculum." *Hunter College*. <http://rwc.hunter.cuny.edu/wac/cuny-creates-wac.html> June 14, 2010.

Coe, Richard, Lorelei Lingard, and Tatiana Teslenko, eds. *The Rhetoric and Ideology of Genre: Strategies for Stability and Change*. Cresskill, NJ: Hampton, 2002. Print.

Cope, Bill, and Mary Kalantzis. *The Powers of Literacy: A Genre Approach to Teaching Writing*. Pittsburgh: U of Pittsburgh P, 1993. Print.

Cripps, Michael, Linda Stanley, Mary Soliday, and Kate Garretson. "Centering WAC at CUNY: Assessing CUNY's WAC Initiative." Annual meeting of the Conference on College Composition and Communication. Palmer House, Chicago. March 23, 2006. Panel presentation.

Currie, Pat. "What Counts as Good Writing? Enculturation and Writing Assessment." Freedman and Medway, *Learning and Teaching Genre* 63–79.

Devitt, Amy. *Writing Genres*. Carbondale: Southern Illinois UP, 2004. Print.

Dias, Patrick, and Anthony Paré, eds. *Transitions: Writing in Academic and Workplace Settings*. Cresskill, NJ: Hampton, 2000. Print.

Dias, Patrick, Aviva Freedman, Peter Medway, and Anthony Paré, eds. *Worlds Apart: Acting and Writing in Academic and Workplace Contexts*. Mahwah, NJ: Erlbaum, 1999. Print.

Downs, Douglas, and Elizabeth Wardle. "Teaching about Writing, Righting Misconceptions: (Re)Envisioning 'First-Year Composition' as 'Introduction to Writing Studies.'" *College Composition and Communication* 58.4 (2007): 552–84. Print.

Durst, Russel K. *Collision Course: Conflict, Negotiation, and Learning in College Composition*. Urbana, IL: NCTE, 1999. Print.

Elbow, Peter. "High Stakes and Low Stakes in Assigning and Responding to Writing." *New Directions for Teaching and Learning* 69 (1997): 5–13. Print.

Fahnestock, Jeanne. "Genre and Rhetorical Craft." *Research in the Teaching of English* 27.3 (1993): 265–71. Print.

Feldman, Ann. *Making Writing Matter: Composition in the Engaged University*. Albany: State U of New York P, 2008. Print.

Fishman, Jenn, Andrea Lunsford, Beth McGregor, and Mark Otuteye. "Performing Writing, Performing Literacy." *College Composition and Communication* 57.2 (2005): 224–52. Print.

Freedman, Aviva. "Show and Tell? The Role of Explicit Teaching in the Learning of New Genres." *Research in the Teaching of English* 27.3 (1993): 222–51. Print.

———. "The What, Where, When, Why and How of Classroom Genres." *Reconceiving Writing, Rethinking Writing Instruction*. Ed. Joseph Petraglia. Mahwah, NJ: Erlbaum, 1995. 121–44. Print.

Freedman, Aviva, and Christine Adam. "Write Where You Are: Situating Learning to Write in University and Workplace Settings." Dias and Paré 31–60.

Freedman, Aviva, and Peter Medway, eds. *Genre and the New Rhetoric.* London: Taylor, 1995. Print.

———, eds. *Learning and Teaching Genre.* Portsmouth, NH: Boynton, 1994. Print.

Gee, James Paul. *Social Linguistics and Literacies.* 2nd. ed. New York: Routledge, 1996. Print.

Geller, Anne Ellen. "'What's Cool Here?' Collaboratively Learning Biology." Herrington and Moran, *Genre across the Curriculum* 83–105.

Giltrow, Janet. "'Argument' as a Term in Talk about Student Writing." Mitchell and Andrews 129–45.

———. "Genre and the Pragmatic Concept of Background Knowledge." Freedman and Medway, *Genre and the New Rhetoric* 155–78.

———. "Meta-Genre." Coe, Lingard, and Teslenko 187–205.

Giltrow, Janet, and Michele Valiquette. "Genres and Knowledge: Students Writing in the Disciplines." Freedman and Medway, *Learning and Teaching Genre* 47–62.

Gottschalk, Katherine, and Keith Hjortshoj. *The Elements of Teaching Writing: A Resource for Instructors in all Disciplines.* New York: Bedford, 2004. Print.

Greene, Stuart. "Making Sense of My Own Ideas: The Problems of Authorship in a Beginning Writing Classroom." *Written Communication* 12.2 (1995): 186–218. Print.

———. "The Question of Authenticity: Teaching Writing in a First-Year College History of Science Class." *Research in the Teaching of English* 35.4 (2001): 525–69. Print.

Groom, Nicholas. "A Workable Balance: Self and Sources in Argumentative Writing." Mitchell and Andrews 65–73.

Haas, Christina. "Learning to Read Biology: One Student's Rhetorical Development in College." *Written Communication* 11.1 (1994): 43–84. Print.

Halpern, Faye. "The Detail versus the Debate: Literature, Argument, and First-year Writing." *Integrating Literature and Writing Instruction: First-Year English, Humanities Core Courses, Seminars.* Ed. Judith Anderson and Christine Farris. New York: MLA, 2007. 135–49. Print.

Henriksen, Erin, Margaret Linton, Tim McCormack, Michaela Rome, Rob Wallace, and Mary Soliday. *Innovative Teaching at City College: A Writing across the Disciplines Handbook for City College Faculty.* 2002. 1-36. Print.

Herrington, Anne. "Composing One's Self in a Discipline: Students' and Teachers' Negotiations." *Constructing Rhetorical Education.* Ed. Marie Secor and Davida Charney. Carbondale: Southern Illinois UP, 1992. 91–115. Print.

———. "Teaching, Writing, and Learning: A Naturalistic Study of Writing in an Undergraduate Literature Course." *Advances in Writing Research: Writing in Academic Disciplines*. Ed. David Jolliffe. Vol. 2. Norwood, NJ: Ablex, 1988. 133–66. Print.

Herrington, Anne, and Charles Moran, eds. *Genre across the Curriculum*. Logan: Utah State UP, 2005. Print.

———, eds. *Writing, Teaching, and Learning in the Disciplines*. New York: MLA, 1992. Print.

Herrington, Anne, and Deborah Cadman. "Peer Review and Revising in an Anthropology Course: Lessons for Learning." *College Composition and Communication* 42.2 (1991): 184–99. Print.

Herrington, Anne, and Marcia Curtis. *Persons in Process: Four Stories of Writing and Personal Development in College*. Urbana, IL: NCTE, 2000. Print.

Hilgers, Thomas, Ann Shea Bayer, Monica Stitt-Bergh, and Megumi Taniguchi. "Doing More Than 'Thinning Out the Herd': How Eighty-Two College Seniors Perceived Writing-Intensive Classes." *Research in the Teaching of English* 29.1 (1995): 59–87. Print.

Hilgers, Thomas, Edna Lardizabal Hussey, and Monica Stitt-Bergh. "'As you're writing, you have these epiphanies': What College Students Say about Writing and Learning in Their Majors." *Written Communication* 16.3 (1999): 317–53. Print.

Hunston, Susan, and Geoff Thompson, eds. *Evaluation in Text: Authorial Stance and the Construction of Discourse*. Oxford: Oxford UP, 2000. Print.

Hunt, Doug. *Misunderstanding the Assignment: Teenage Students, College Writing, and the Pains of Growth*. Portsmouth, NH: Boynton, 2002. Print.

Iconis, Rosemary. "Writing across the Curriculum at the City University of New York." *Journal of College Teaching and Learning* 3.4 (2006): 1–5. Web. <http://www.cluteinstitute-onlinejournals.com/PDFs/200671.pdf>.

Johns, Ann, ed. *Genre in the Classroom: Multiple Perspectives*. Mahwah, NJ: Erlbaum, 2002. Print.

———. "Teaching Classroom and Authentic Genres: Initiating Students into Academic Cultures and Discourses." Belcher and Braine 277–291.

Jones, Robert, and Joseph J. Comprone. "Where Do We Go Next in Writing across the Curriculum?" *College Composition and Communication* 44.1 (1993): 59–68. Print.

Journet, Debra. "Boundary Rhetoric and Disciplinary Genres: Redrawing the Maps in Interdisciplinary Writing." *Genre and Writing: Issues, Arguments, Alternatives*. Ed. Wendy Bishop and Hans Ostrom. Portsmouth, NH: Boynton. 56–69. Print.

Kaufer, David, and Richard Young. "Writing in the Content Areas: Some Theoretical Complexities." *Theory and Practice in the Teaching of Writing*. Ed. Lee Odell, Carbondale: Southern Illinois UP, 1993. 71–104. Print.

Kiniry, Malcolm, and Ellen Strenski. "Sequencing Expository Writing: A Recursive Approach." *College Composition and Communication* 36.2 (1985): 191–202. Print.

Kipling, Kim, and Richard Murphy. *Symbiosis: Writing and an Academic Culture*. Boston: Boynton, 1992. Print.

Kirscht, Judy, Rhonda Levine, and John Reiff. "Evolving Paradigms: WAC and the Rhetoric of Inquiry." *College Composition and Communication* 45.3 (1994): 369–80. Print.

Lane, Suzanne. "Invention and Arrangement: Engineering an Essay." Annual meeting of the Conference on College Composition and Communication. Hilton, New Orleans. April 3, 2008. Panel presentation.

Lave, Jean, and Etienne Wenger. *Situated Learning: Legitimate Peripheral Participation*. Cambridge: Cambridge UP, 1991. Print.

LeFevre, Karen Burke. *Invention as a Social Act*. Carbondale: Southern Illinois UP, 1987. Print.

Leki, Ilona. "Good Writing: I Know It When I See It." Belcher and Braine 23–46.

———. "Living through College Literacy: Nursing in a Second Language." *Written Communication* 20.1 (2003): 81–98. Print.

Light, Richard. *Making the Most of College: Students Speak Their Minds*. Cambridge: Harvard UP, 2001. Print.

Lillis, Theresa. "Whose 'Common Sense'? Essayist Literacy and the Institutional Practice of Mystery." *Students Writing in the University: Cultural and Epistemological Issues*. Ed. Carys Jones, Joan Turner, and Brian Street. Amsterdam: Benjamins, 1999. 127–47. Print.

Lingard, Lorelei, and Richard Haber. "Learning Medical Talk: How the Apprenticeship Complicates Current Explicit/Tacit Debates in Genre Instruction." Coe, Lingard, and Teslenko 155–70.

MacDonald, Susan Peck, and Charles Cooper. "Contributions of Academic and Dialogic Journals to Writing about Literature." Herrington and Moran, *Writing, Teaching, and Learning in the Disciplines* 137–55.

Mallonee, Barbara, and John Breihan. "Responding to Students' Drafts: Interdisciplinary Consensus." *College Composition and Communication* 36.2 (1985): 213–31. Print.

Marsella, Joy, Thomas Hilgers, and Clemence McLaren. "How Students Handle Writing Assignments: A Study of Eighteen Responses in Six Disciplines." Herrington and Moran, *Writing, Teaching, and Learning in the Disciplines* 174–88.

McCarthy, Lucille. "A Stranger in Strange Lands: A College Student Writing across the Curriculum." *Research in the Teaching of English* 21.3 (1987): 233–65. Print.

McKeon, Michael. *The Origins of the English Novel: 1600–1740.* 1987. Baltimore: Johns Hopkins UP, 2002. Print.

McLeod, Susan, and Elaine Maimon. "Clearing the Air: WAC Myths and Realities." *College English* 62.5 (May 2000): 573–83. Print.

McLeod, Susan, Eric Miraglia, Margot Soven, and Christopher Thaiss, eds. *WAC for the New Millennium: Strategies for Continuing Writing-across-the-Curriculum Programs.* Urbana, IL: NCTE, 2001. Print.

Miller, Carolyn. "Genre as Social Action." *Quarterly Journal of Speech* 70 (1984): 151–67. Print.

———. "Rhetorical Community: The Cultural Basis of Genre." Freedman and Medway, *Genre and the New Rhetoric* 67–77.

Mitchell, Sally, and Richard Andrews, eds. *Learning to Argue in Higher Education.* Portsmouth, NH: Boynton, 2000. Print.

Monroe, Jonathan, ed. *Local Knowledges, Local Practices: Writing in the Disciplines at Cornell.* Pittsburgh: U of Pittsburgh P, 2003. Print.

Murray, Patricia. "Teachers as Readers, Readers as Teachers." *Encountering Student Texts: Interpretive Issues in Reading Student Writing.* Ed. Bruce Lawson, Susan Ryan, and Ross Winterowd. Urbana, IL: NCTE, 1989. 73–85. Print.

*National Survey of Student Engagement.* Bloomington: Indiana University Center for Postsecondary Research, 2008. Print.

Nelms, Gerald, and Ronda Leathers Dively. "Perceived Roadblocks to Transferring Knowledge from First-Year Composition to Writing—Intensive Major Courses: A Pilot Study." *WPA: Writing Program Administration* 31.1–2 (2007): 214–40. Print.

Odell, Lee, and Dixie Goswami, eds. *Writing in Nonacademic Settings.* New York: Guilford, 1986. Print.

Paltridge, Brian. *Genre and the Language Learning Classroom.* Ann Arbor: U of Michigan P, 2001. Print.

Peak, Ken, and Mark Waldo. "On Assigning and Assessing Students' Prose: A Discipline-based Approach." *Journal of Criminal Justice Education* 8.1 (1997): 75–80. Print.

Penrose, Ann, and Cheryl Geisler. "Reading and Writing without Authority." *College Composition and Communication* 45.4 (1994): 505–20. Print.

Prior, Paul. *Writing/Disciplinarity: A Sociohistoric Account of Literate Activity in the Academy.* Mahwah, NJ: Erlbaum, 1998. Print.

Russell, David, and Arturo Yañez. "'Big Picture People Rarely Become Historians': Genre Systems and the Contradictions of General Education." Bazerman and Russell 331–61.

Schon, Donald. *The Reflective Practitioner: How Professionals Think in Action*. New York: Basic, 1983. Print.

Segal, Judy, Anthony Paré, Doug Brent, and Douglas Vipond. "The Researcher as Missionary: Problems with Rhetoric and Reform in the Disciplines." *College Composition and Communication* 50.1 (1998): 71–90. Print.

Segall, Mary, and Robert Smart, eds. *Direct from the Disciplines: Writing across the Curriculum*. Portsmouth, NH: Boynton, 2005. Print.

Shaughnessy, Mina. *Errors and Expectations*. 1977. New York: Oxford UP, 1979. Print.

Smart, Graham. "Reinventing Expertise: Experienced Writers in the Workplace Encounter a New Genre." Dias and Paré 223–52.

Smit, David. *The End of Composition Studies*. Carbondale: Southern Illinois UP, 2004. Print.

Smith, Summer. "The Role of Technical Expertise in Engineering and Writing Teachers' Evaluations of Students' Writing." *Written Communication* 20.1 (2003): 37–80. Print.

Soliday, Mary. "A Comparative Study of Writing in a General Education Course." Annual meeting of Conference on College Composition and Communication. Hilton, New York City. March 26, 2007. Panel presentation.

———. "Mapping Genres in a Science of Society Course." Herrington and Moran, *Genre across the Curriculum* 65–82.

———. "Reading Student Writing with Anthropologists: Stance and Judgment in College Writing." *College Composition and Communication* 56.1 (2004): 72–93. Print.

———. "Shifting Roles in Classroom Tutoring: Cultivating the Art of Boundary Crossing." *Writing Center Journal* 16.1 (1995): 59–73. Print.

Sommers, Nancy, and Laura Saltz. "The Novice as Expert: Writing the Freshman Year." *College Composition and Communication* 56.1 (2004): 124–49. Print.

Soven, Margot. "Curriculum-based Peer Tutors and WAC." McLeod, Miraglia, Soven, and Thaiss 200–223.

———. *What the Writing Tutor Needs to Know*. Boston: Thomson, 2006. Print.

Spilka, Rachel, ed. *Writing in the Workplace: New Research Perspectives*. Carbondale: Southern Illinois UP, 1993. Print.

Sternglass, Marilyn. *Time to Know Them: A Longitudinal Study of Writing and Learning at the College Level*. Mahwah, NJ: Erlbaum, 1997. Print.

Stockton, Sharon. "Writing in History: Narrating the Subject of Time." *Written Communication* 12.1 (1995): 47–73. Print.

Strachan, Wendy. *Writing-Intensive: Becoming W-Faculty in a New Writing Curriculum*. Logan: Utah State UP, 2008. Print.

Tardy, Christine. "A Genre System View of the Funding of Academic Research." *Written Communication* 20.1 (2003): 7–36. Print.

Thaiss, Christopher. "Theory in WAC: Where Have We Been, Where Are We Going?" McLeod, Miraglia, Soven, and Thaiss 299–325.

———, ed. *Writing to Learn: Essays and Reflections on Writing across the Curriculum*. Dubuque: Kendall, 1983. Print.

Thaiss, Christopher, and Terry Myers Zawacki. *Engaged Writers and Dynamic Disciplines: Research on the Academic Writing Life*. Portsmouth, NH: Heinemann, 2006. Print.

———. "How Portfolios for Proficiency Help Shape a WAC Program." Yancey and Huot 79–96.

Thomas, Sharon, Julie Bevins, and Mary Ann Crawford. "The Portfolio Project: Sharing Our Stories." *Writing Center Research: Extending the Conversation*. Ed. Paula Gillespie, Alice Gillam, Lady Falls Brown, and Byron Stay. Mahwah, NJ: Erlbaum, 2002. 149–66. Print.

Vande Kopple, William. "Metadiscourse, Discourse, and Issues in Composition and Rhetoric." *Discourse Studies in Composition*. Ed. Ellen Barton and Gail Stygall. Cresskill, NJ: Hampton, 2002. 91–113. Print.

Waldo, Mark. *Demythologizing Language Difference in the Academy: Establishing Discipline-based Writing Programs*. Mahwah, NJ: Erlbaum, 2004. Print.

Walvoord, Barbara E., and John R. Breihan. "Arguing and Debating: Breihan's History Course." Walvoord and McCarthy 97–143.

Walvoord, Barbara E., Linda Hunt, H. Fil Dowling Jr., and Joan McMahon. *In the Long Run: A Study of Faculty in Three Writing-across-the-Curriculum Programs*. Urbana, IL: NCTE, 1997. Print.

Walvoord, Barbara E., and Lucille Parkinson McCarthy. *Thinking and Writing in College: A Naturalistic Study of Students in Four Disciplines*. In collaboration with Virginia Johnson Anderson, John R. Breihan, Susan Miller Robison, and A. Kimbrough Sherman. Urbana, IL: NCTE, 1990. Print.

Wardle, Elizabeth. "'Mutt Genres' and the Goal of FYC: Can We Help Students Write the Genres of the University?" *College Composition and Communication* 60.4 (2009): 765–89. Print.

———. "Understanding 'Transfer' from FYC: Preliminary Results of a Longitudinal Study." *WPA: Writing Program Administration* 31.1–2 (2007): 65–85. Print.

Wenger, Etienne. *Communities of Practice: Learning, Meaning, and Identity*. Cambridge: Cambridge UP, 1998. Print.

Williams, Joseph, and Gregory Colomb. "The Case for Explicit Teaching: Why What You Don't Know Won't Help You." *Research in the Teaching of English* 27.3 (1993): 252–64. Print.

Winsor, Dorothy. "Genre and Activity Systems: The Role of Documentation in Maintaining and Changing Engineering Activity Systems." *Written Communication* 16.2 (1999): 200–224. Print.

———. *Writing like an Engineer: A Rhetorical Education*. Mahwah, NJ: Erlbaum, 1996. Print.

Yancey, Kathleen, and Brian Huot, eds. *Assessing Writing across the Curriculum: Diverse Approaches and Practices*. Vol. 1. Greenwich, CT: Ablex, 1997. Print.

Young, Art, and Toby Fulwiler. *Writing across the Disciplines: Research into Practice*. Portsmouth, NH: Boynton, 1986. Print.

# INDEX

**Mary Soliday** is a professor of English and the director of writing across the curriculum at San Francisco State University, where she teaches writing and literature courses. She is the author of *The Politics of Remediation* (2002), winner of the 2004 4Cs Outstanding Book Award.

## CCCC STUDIES IN WRITING & RHETORIC

*Edited by Joseph Harris, Duke University*

The aim of the CCCC Studies in Writing & Rhetoric (SWR) series is to influence how writing gets taught at the college level. The methods of studies vary from the critical to historical to linguistic to ethnographic, and their authors draw on work in various fields that inform composition—including rhetoric, communication, education, discourse analysis, psychology, cultural studies, and literature. Their focuses are similarly diverse—ranging from individual writers and teachers, to classrooms and communities and curricula, to analyses of the social, political, and material contexts of writing and its teaching. Still, all SWR volumes try in some way to inform the practice of writing students, teachers, or administrators. Their approach is synthetic, their style concise and pointed. Complete manuscripts run from 40,000 to 50,000 words, or about 150 to 200 pages. Authors should imagine their work in the hands of writing teachers as well as on library shelves.

SWR was one of the first scholarly book series to focus on the teaching of writing. It was established in 1980 by the Conference on College Composition and Communication (CCCC) to promote research in the emerging field of writing studies. Since its inception, the series has been copublished by Southern Illinois University Press. As the field has grown, the research sponsored by SWR has continued to articulate the commitment of CCCC to supporting the work of writing teachers as reflective practitioners and intellectuals. For a list of previous SWR books, see the SWR link on the SIU Press website at www.siupress.com.

We are eager to identify influential work in writing and rhetoric as it emerges. We thus ask authors to send us project proposals that clearly situate their work in the field and show how they aim to redirect our ongoing conversations about writing and its teaching. Proposals should include an overview of the project, a brief annotated table of contents, and a sample chapter. They should not exceed 10,000 words.

To submit a proposal or to contact the series editor, please go to http://uwp.aas.duke.edu/cccc/swr/.